We Almost Made It!

Published in Hampton, VA, by Fruition Publishing Concierge Services. Fruition Publishing Concierge Services is a division of Alesha Brown, LLC.

Fruition Publishing Concierge Services can bring authors to your live event. For more information or to book an event, visit Fruition Publishing Concierge Services at

www.FruitionPublishing.com

ISBN: 978-1-954486-10-2 Paperback

ISBN: 978-1-954486-09-6 eBook

Library of Congress Control Number: 2021911964

DEDICATION

This book is dedicated to:

Our Mothers: Ms. Sallie Mae Calvie and Ms. Agnes Pope.

All my Aunts: Not only those pictured in this book.

My Godmother: Mrs. Leila Pope.

All Family, Friends, and Supporters: To our family members and friends, too many to name, that have supported us, encouraged us, mentored us, nurtured us, and befriended us along the way.

Ms. Sallie

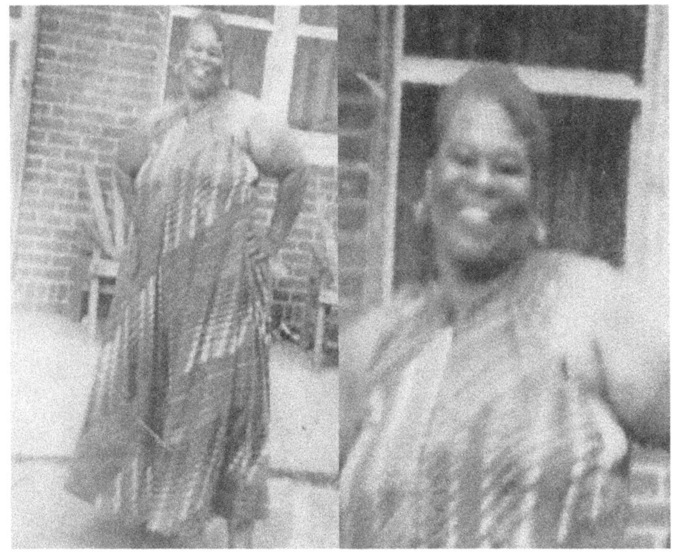

PREFACE

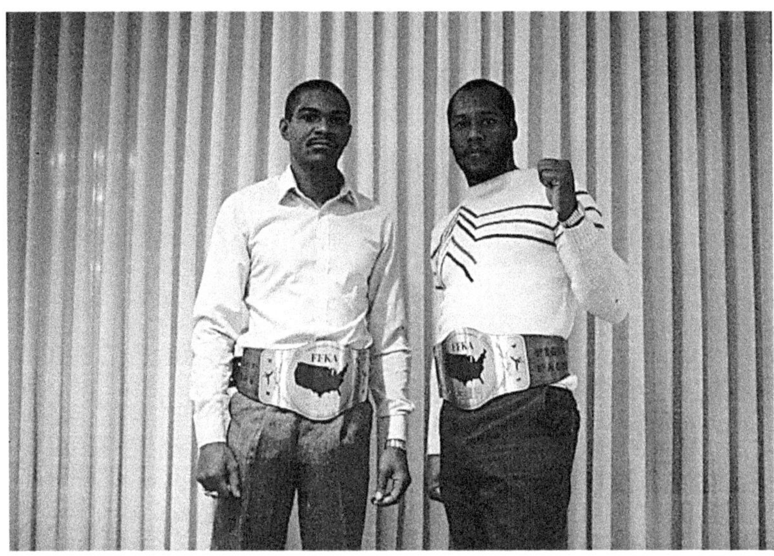

Let me start by introducing myself to those that may not know me. My name is Sylvester Cash, Sr., and I want to thank you for taking the time to read my story, **We Almost Made It**.

This story in no way is meant to embarrass, make fun of, point fingers at, destroy the reputation of, tell about, cast a shadow over the legacy, destroy the credibility of, demean the character of, or get even with anyone. Others in my circle may have seen it another way and others may feel slighted. I apologize to those but this is my story told the way I saw it.

I began thinking about and writing this story more than 20 years ago. It was originally based on my relationship with my good friend and Sensei, Leroy "Superfeet" Taylor. I was excited about all the good community work that we were doing and how far we had come in the art of karate. At that time, my focus was much clearer than now. So I must tell this story while I can.

I planned to write our life stories in parallel, because I felt that both of us, having been raised similarly in Baltimore City, needed to tell our stories. My thoughts were more about Leroy than myself, because of his unselfish giving of his time and talents to his community along with his accomplishments. I felt, and still feel, that his story needs to be told.

Leroy is a pillar of the community; one that should never be forgotten. Because of my limited interviewing and writing skills, I felt that I could not do justice in any story I wrote to honor him. So, this story has taken a different course. I decided that it would be best to attempt to honor him by introducing my family to him. I want to show the great influence he has had on my life since becoming a Martial Artist.

My other reason for changing the course of this book was my lack of knowledge of my family. I grew up only knowing a small amount of history of the Pope side of my family. That portion was only about my Grand Father, Sidney Pope. I know even less about the Cash side of my family, only learning that when I started spending more time with my father after my mother died.

We Almost Made It has also been written that I may leave my children, grandchildren, great-grandchildren and the other off-springs from my loins, with the written knowledge of Sylvester Cash, Sr. I want my offspring to not only know my name, but where I come from, the type of man I was, and the roads I traveled in my life.

To those of you that I have just met, I hope to inspire you never to give up on yourself, your dreams, or your goals in life. Your Great Creator put them in your head for you to see what lies ahead waiting for you. Keep the "FAITH; you can make it!

-Sylvester Cash, Sr.

Table of Contents

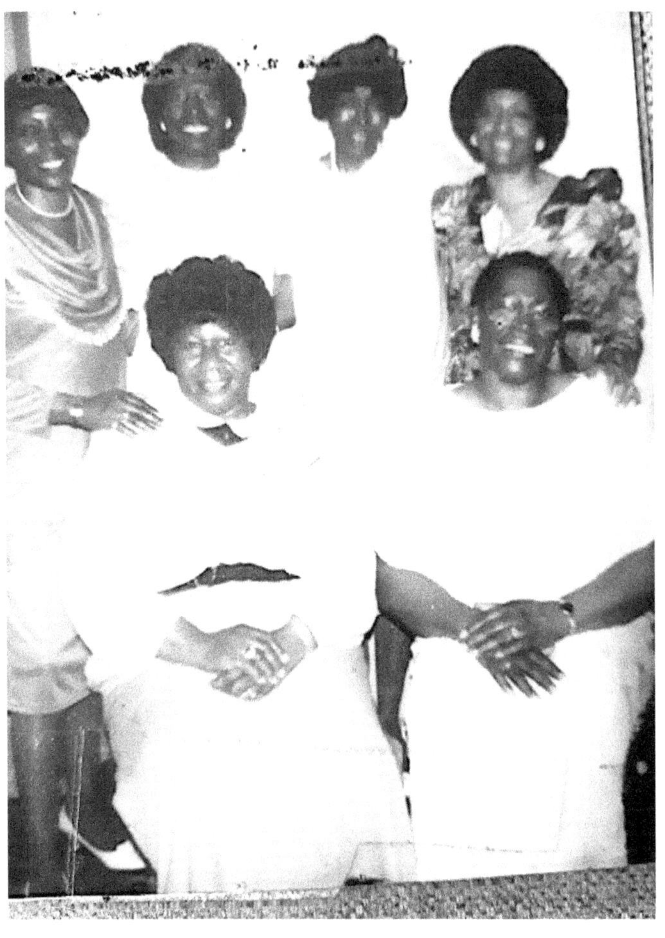

Front (L to R): Aunt Jeanne Mae and Momma

Back (L to R): Aunts Lula Bea, Evelyn, Gladys, and Leila (My Godmother)

See all photos including color versions at sylvestercash.com.

Chapter 1

Grand Master Leroy "Superfeet" Taylor

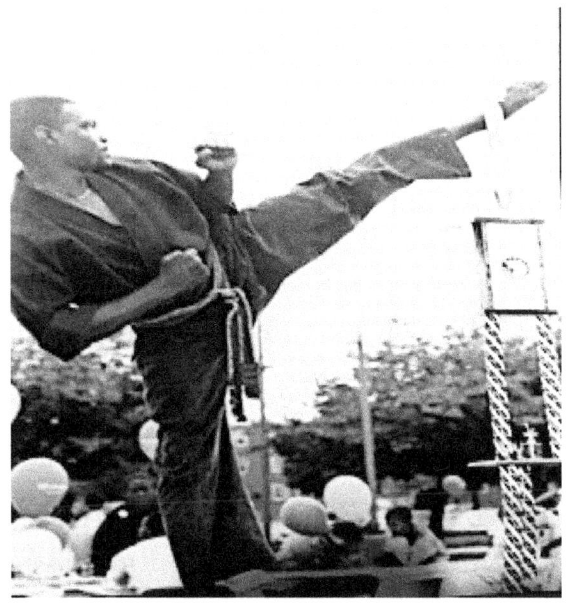

We Almost Made It is an account of two Black men growing up in the slums of Baltimore City, Maryland. We met in 1977 at the Murphy Homes Recreation Center. This center provided a refuge, sanctuary, and hope for many Black children from low-income families growing up in the Murphy Homes Projects in Baltimore City.

Those who know me, or who have honored me by choosing to read this book, may still be asking, *Why did he (Cash) write this?* You want to know what made me choose Leroy Calvie Taylor over all of the people that I grew up with, including family members that raised and nurtured me and the men and women that unknowingly helped to shape and mold my life?

- Why not Ferny Dennis who introduced me to Leroy?

- Why not Greg "Speedo" Brown who noticed my potential talent in Full Contact Karate? Who trained and nurtured me through most of my Full Contact Karate career?

- Why not Jerry Boorts, "The White Man" in my corner, that not only got me into the Plumbing and HVAC trades and helped me start my own plumbing business, but also refined my full contact training and boxing skills? He was the one that taught me about life on the other side of the street and how to make it work for me.

- Why not Mr. Charles Johnston, who took a bunch of us young men living in the ghetto, into his mentorship and began teaching us about life on the street and the importance of education? He was my introduction to the Marine Corps. I wanted to be a marine just like him.

Well, there is no real concrete answer as to why I chose this Unsung Hero, Leroy "Superfeet" Taylor, a product of Baltimore's Murphy Homes Projects highlighted in this manuscript. All I know is that in 1977, I was sent into his life by a force more powerful than any other force I know. From that first day, he has always been a great inspiration to me. The roads that we traveled have not been easy and, even when we did not have, we found a way.

I would watch how calm he was in the face of turmoil. I watched when he won the cash prizes and gave most of it to the kids that did not have and the competitors that spent their last in the hope of winning the cash prize that day. I learned first-hand from that teacher/student relationship. When he and Speedo would reach the finals, one would bow out to the other. Sensei Leroy being the student; Sensei Speedo being the Instructor. The money always went to a good cause.

After I earned my Black Belt and became a top competitor in the Light Heavyweight division, I was able to eliminate the upper competitors and make their jobs easier. We were so good that we would go to a couple of tournaments a day during the weekend. We would arrive in time to compete for the Black Belt division. We would win the money and go to the next tournament in the area. This was almost like a part-time job.

I was him: I listened to the things he did not say and I watched the results. Even when we were broke, it was still not about the money. He had offers to leave Baltimore and be sponsored, but that meant not only leaving his students but selling his soul. I think it was ingrained in our upbringing that our integrity was worth a lot more than the titles and money. Sensei never let it get the best of him. As I alluded to earlier, this shaped me as a professional competitor and made me a better man.

I want to make sure that people know and remember Leroy "Superfeet" Taylor as a great athlete, a great human being, a great Father, an incredible instructor, and a great friend to all that crossed his path. I especially want the people of

Baltimore to not forget what this Brother brought and gave to children and adults alike within our communities. Leroy touched so many lives there. I want those after us to know his story and make it a part of the history of our community and culture.

First of all, we both grew up in a single-parent household: him in the projects of Murphy Homes and me in the Mondawmin area of Baltimore City. In the times we came up in, the odds were that we would not make it out of the ghetto. Both of us being a product of Frederick Douglass Senior High School and the Community College of Baltimore (CCB), our education was always questioned. Both of us being "champions" in our own right, we have endured the test of time.

I once had a professor at a predominantly white college in Baltimore make an example of me with another professor by challenging my writing skills. He asked the question: *What junior college did you attend?* I said CCB and his response was: *See? I told you.* We all know what that meant!

Another time I met with a representative of a fight promoter, who came to meet me to sign a contract for a fight. I told him that I had to go to class after I met with him, and his response was: *Oh, you are studying to get your GED?* My response was: *No, I am a junior in college!* I knew then that my educational development was questionable, but I refused to let their thoughts hold me back. I started taking advantage of the tutoring programs they had and started reading and writing more.

Unlike myself, I am happy to say, Leroy was able to use his athletic skills to put his name in the record books of CCB through wrestling. He became the first to win a major junior college wrestling championship for CCB. It was the beginning of him putting his name in the record books as *champion.*

I remember in karate class, he would spar and wrestle every student and never get tired! At karate tournaments, he would compete in and win both the kata and sparring divisions, and this continued for over 40 plus years. Most of us would just do one or the other, kata or sparring, usually not both. That inspired me to work harder and also taught me what it meant to set an example for my students to follow. Eventually, I started placing in both events.

Finally, through all of his hard work, Leroy's talents paid off at the ultimate level of karate: Professional Karate Association (PKA) Full Contact Karate. When he fought for the Professional Karate Association Light Welterweight Title, the other side had to deal with it! Though it was not said in open conversation, he was not supposed to win, but he prevailed and became the PKA Light Welterweight World Champion. He was the first Professional Full Contact Karate pugilist from Baltimore City, still living in Baltimore City, to ever win a bona fide World Championship. Once again, Leroy had his name in the record book as *champion.*

One evening, on the streets of Baltimore, a thug/person of unsound mind and bad intentions tried to end his life. That was indeed a frightening time for him as well as his family, friends, and the community he served. After a long period of therapy and rest, Leroy went back to teaching karate and competing nationally.

There are so many people's lives he has touched including mine. I wish I could write about every one of them. If I started describing things that these personalities said and did, you would definitely be able to say: *Yep; I know somebody like that,* or *I know what he is talking about.* We all have those family members, neighbors, teachers, instructors, friends, associates, co-workers, and others that cross our paths, whom we would like to tell the world about. I truly believe the saying: *People come into your life for a reason, a season, for a short time, or a lifetime.*

Well, I sense Leroy came into my life for a reason and a lifetime. I still have not figured it all out yet, but I have this sentiment deep down inside that his story needs to be told! The way I see it, the *hood* is comprised of so many talents, dreams, ambitions, and tragedies that will never be told. When they are told, they are just blurbs on the TV or in the newspapers. Then we sit and cry over what they meant to us and the community and what we should have done to help them. Shame on us!

We as *people of color* have so much history that has been lost and I do not want his story to be left untold. However, as I began to write this, I realized that I do not know as much about Sensei Leroy as I thought I did. I realized writing this that I am not the one to tell his narrative. I can only talk about what I observed and know through our many years of conversations and travel.

I can tell you that we were at each other's wedding. Our Moms would work together to support our programs. Our older children kind of grew up together. Because he is a private person and I respect his privacy, it is hard for me to extract information from Leroy that I might share with the world. What I know is only the tip of the iceberg, so I will not be able to give him his just due. As I said before, there is more to his story than I can give you in this one book, but I hope and pray that somebody tells it!

I Love and have Great Respect for you, My Brother, and My Sensei!

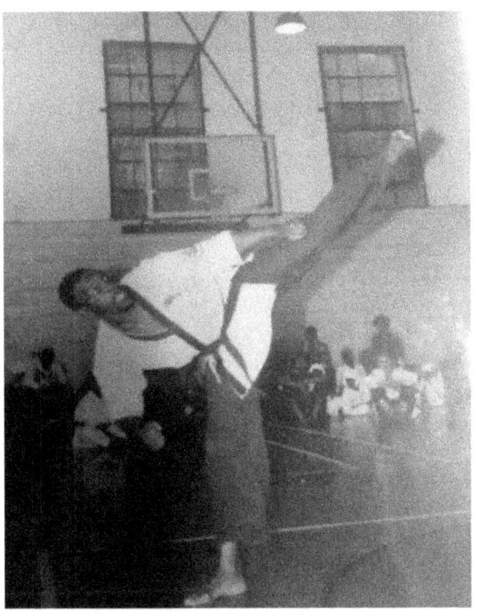

There are extraordinary individuals that emerge and are never recognized outside of their communities. Our children and future generations are rarely exposed to their contributions or activities. In turn, these Unsung Heroes' names and ordeals are only mentioned in belated social gatherings, mainly funerals. Instead of children choosing their heroes from among those that have advanced their community, they are forced to choose heroes that they will never see in their neighborhoods and will never know personally. To me that is SAD!

There are many boxing champions from Baltimore who have made it to the history books. Let's start with Joe Gans, known as the *Old Master*, who was the first African-American World Boxing Champion of the 20th century, reigning continuously as World Lightweight Champion from 1902 to 1908. He has been rated the greatest lightweight boxer of all-times.

Then there was Dwight Muhammad Qawi, (born Dwight Braxton), who was born in Baltimore City but grew up in Camden, New Jersey. He held world champion titles in two weight classes: the WBC's Ring Magazine Light Heavyweight titles from 1981 to 1983 and the WBA's Cruiserweight title from 1985 to 1986.

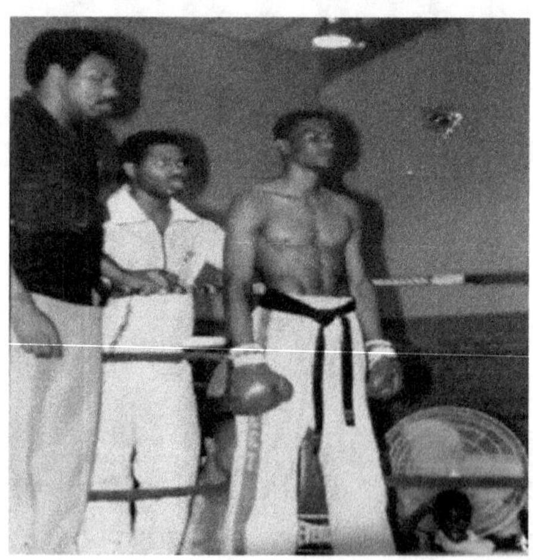

Former Heavyweight Contender, Larry Middleton, and Golden Gloves Champion, David Spriwell

Hasim Sharif Rahman, who competed from 1994 to 2014, was a two-time World Heavyweight Champion, having unified the WBC, IBF, IBO, and lineal titles in 2001 and the WBC title again from 2005 to 2006. Gervonta Davis was a two-time Super Featherweight World champion, having held the WBA (Super) title from 2018 to 2019 and the IBF title in 2017. I feel that Leroy "Superfeet" Taylor's name should be given the same honor for his achievements in Professional Full Contact Karate. He should be given his rightful recognition in this pugilistic sport.

This section is about my Unsung Hero and the relationship we developed along the way. It talks a little about our struggles and setbacks competing in karate and Full Contact Karate arenas. Every competitor's goal is to become the best in the world at what they participate in and practice and Leroy did just that!

When I first met Leroy, I realized his first concern was for his family and students. Even though he was poor himself, he would tell you what the dues were but would never come to you and ask for a penny. If you wanted to go to a tournament and didn't have the money, he would find a way to get you there, get you in, and make sure you had something to eat. I've seen him take the money he won at the tournament that day and pay the promoter for his students. He never turned anyone down that wanted to learn karate or kickboxing. I've seen competitors come to ask him to train them and to tell of the financial bind they were in. He would give them part of his winnings.

He and I used to train in his mother's living room in Murphy Homes at 7:00 in the morning before we went to school or work. We did this for over two years. I would train six days a week, sometimes twice a day. Then I started competing in all the tournaments. As a result, I earned my Black Belt in a little less than three years. It was his first Black Belt!

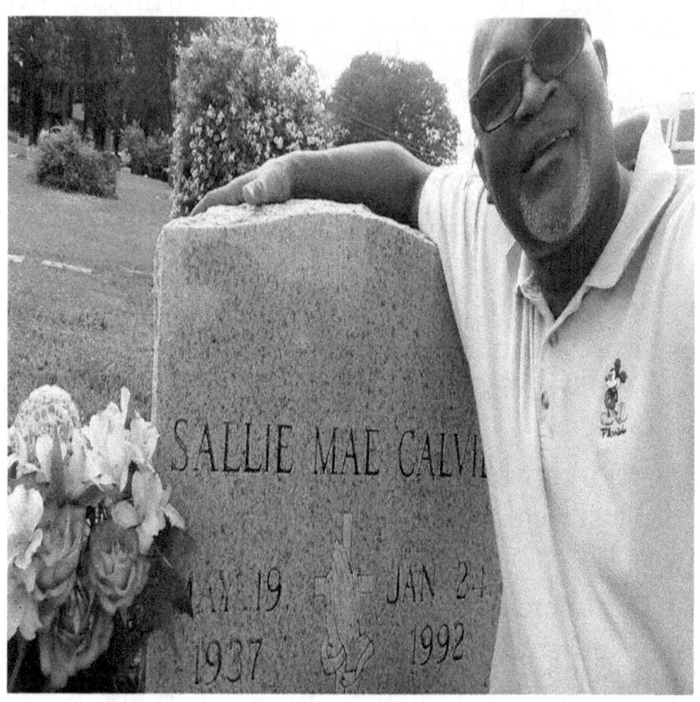

Leroy Calvie grew up in the Murphy Homes Community of Baltimore City and was born in July 1957. Leroy taught karate from 1970 to 1992 at the Murphy Homes Recreation Center. During those times, Murphy Homes had a reputation of being one of the most dangerous areas in Baltimore City to live in or even think about visiting. Afterward, he opened his own school on the second floor of Madison Avenue and Eutaw Street from 1992 to 2008. He moved to Sharp Street Church from 2010 to 2018, then to Woodlawn.

His mother, Ms. Sallie Mae Calvie, loved her children very much and supported them in their endeavors. Even though she worked long hours, she made time to come to the major karate events and Full Contact Karate bouts they were in. Ms. Sallie's family was known as a Karate family and not to be messed with. They were all quiet and respectful but you did not want to get on the wrong side of them. You just did not fight one of them, but you fought the whole family.

Ms. Sallie became a mother and confidant for every one of Leroy's students. Ms. Sallie was no-nonsense, but she was easy to talk to and would give it to you straight. She would also give you a hug if she thought you needed it. Ms. Sallie was a great cook and was known for her chicken and fish dinners. Nobody in Baltimore cooked Lake Trout and Oyster Trout fish dinners as good as she did!

There were five children in the Calvie –Taylor family. Betty was the eldest daughter and Leroy the eldest son. Then there was John, Elliott (Bubbles), Sarah, and Jerry.

Leroy had four children to my knowledge: Dawn, Tina, Sean, and his youngest son Darius.

John "The Mallet" Taylor FFKA World Champion with Brothers Bubbles and Leroy

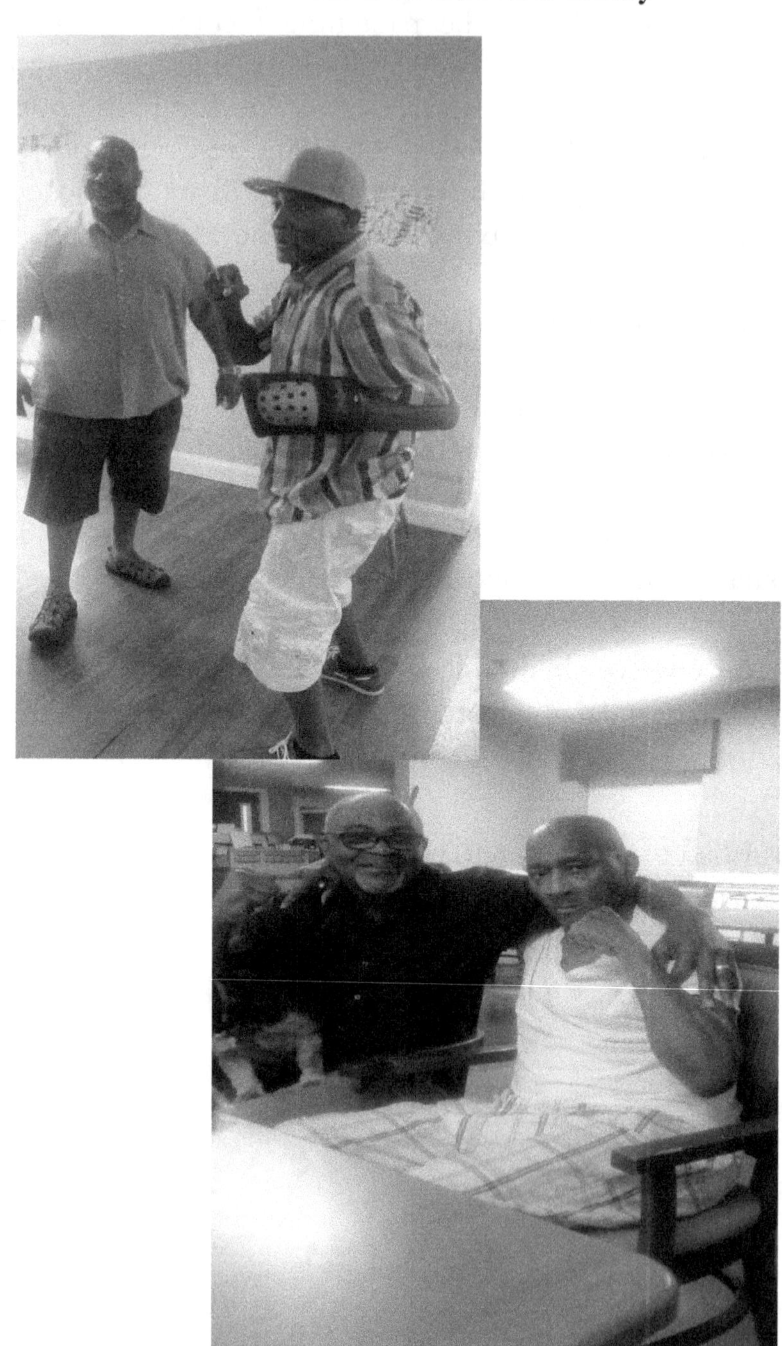

Leroy with Daughters Tina and Dawn

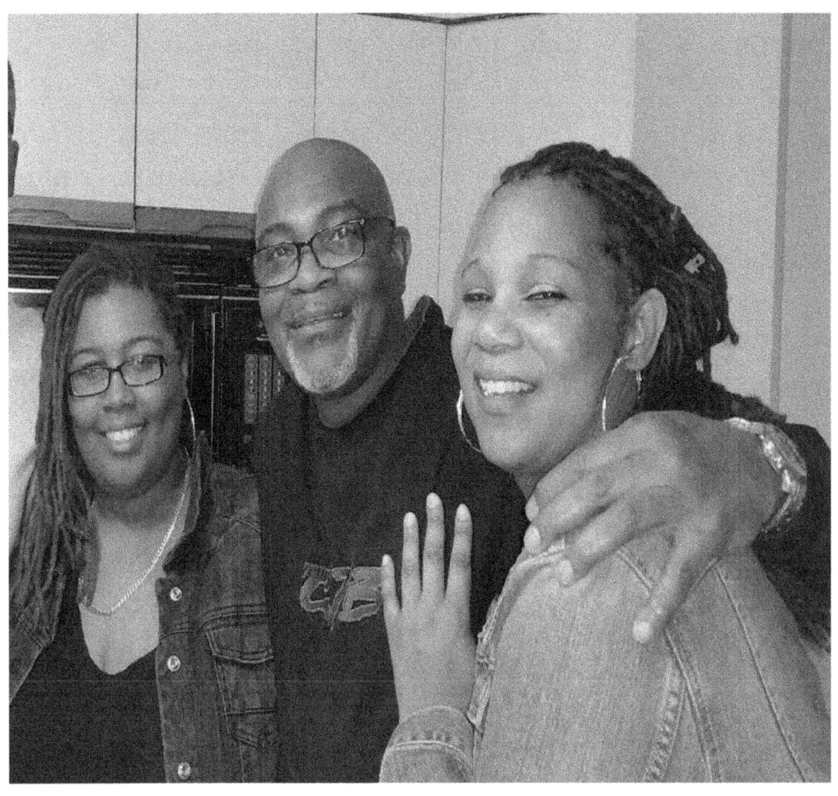

Leroy attended and graduated from Frederick Douglass High School where he excelled in wrestling. He attended the Community College of Baltimore where he joined the wrestling team and became the first person to win a Junior College Wrestling Championship in Baltimore. He also became the first person out of Baltimore to win a World Title Championship in Full Contact Karate.

Leroy Calvie Taylor, known as Leroy "Superfeet" Taylor, taught Karate at the Murphy Homes Recreation Center from the beginning of his adult life for a very small fee, or even free until the center was closed. Even when he established a fee for his students, those that could not pay were never turned away. He was a person that never would ask you for your dues, so if you did not pay that was on you.

As time would have it, we both married and divorced. Our mothers were strong Black women who kept the families together. Both our mothers passed away shortly after we married in the 1990s.

The door finally opened up for Leroy when he defeated Dave Humphries for the FFKA World Welterweight Crown and then they gave him a shot at the vacant PKA Light Welterweight World Title in Canada against Leo Loucks. We knew they thought that Leo would beat Leroy, but being the great competitor Leroy is, he proved them wrong.

Leroy Taylor vs Leo Loucks World Title Fight

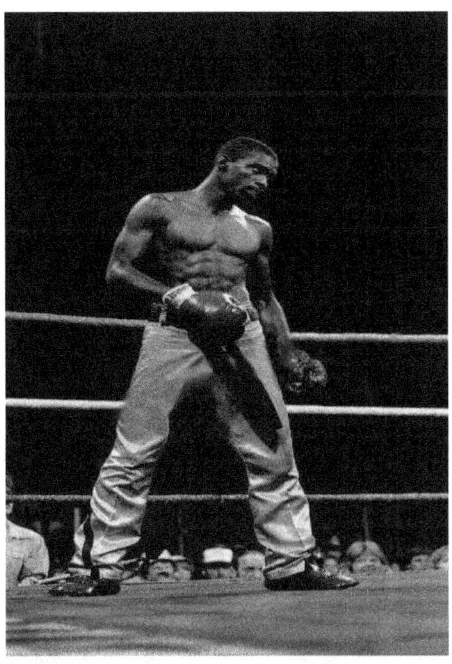

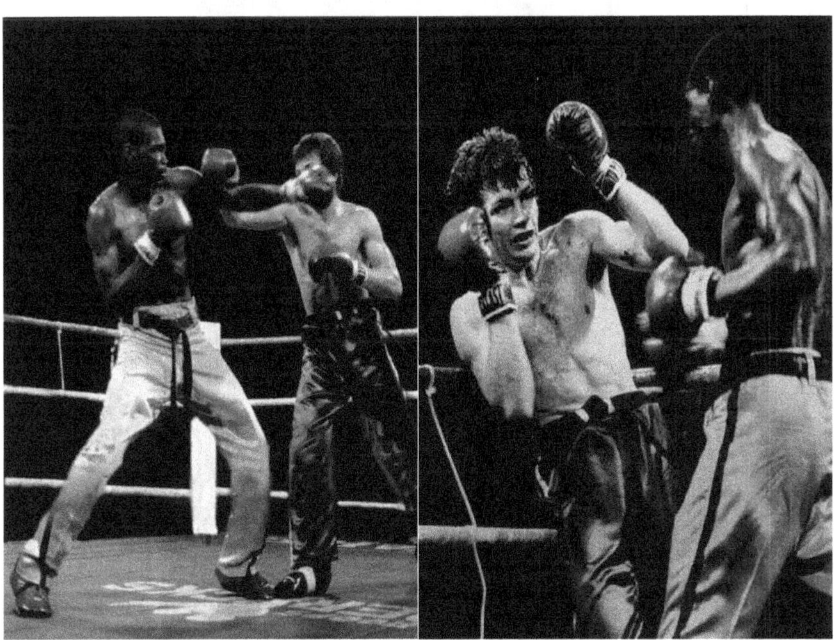

Leroy "Superfeet" Taylor's Victory Celebration against Greg "Speedo" Brown

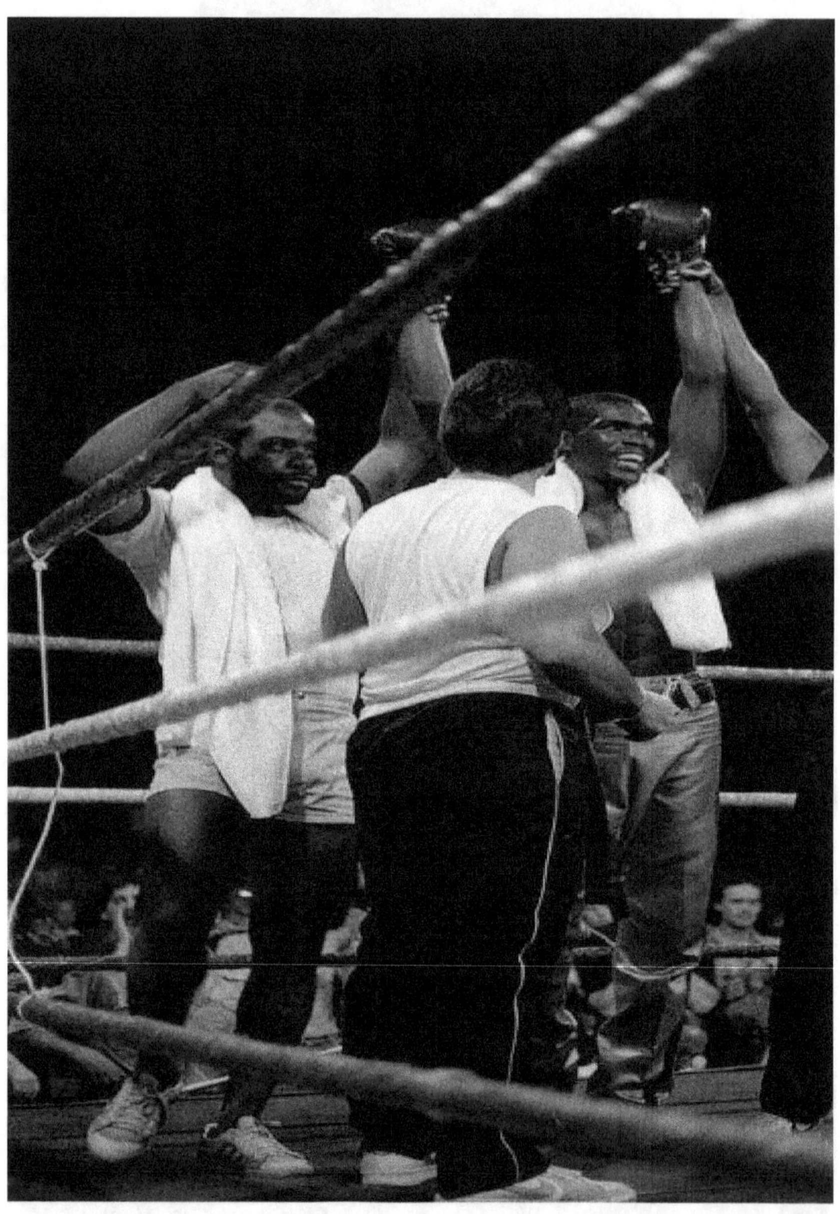

Ms. Sallie, Leroy, Treola, Shawn, Cash

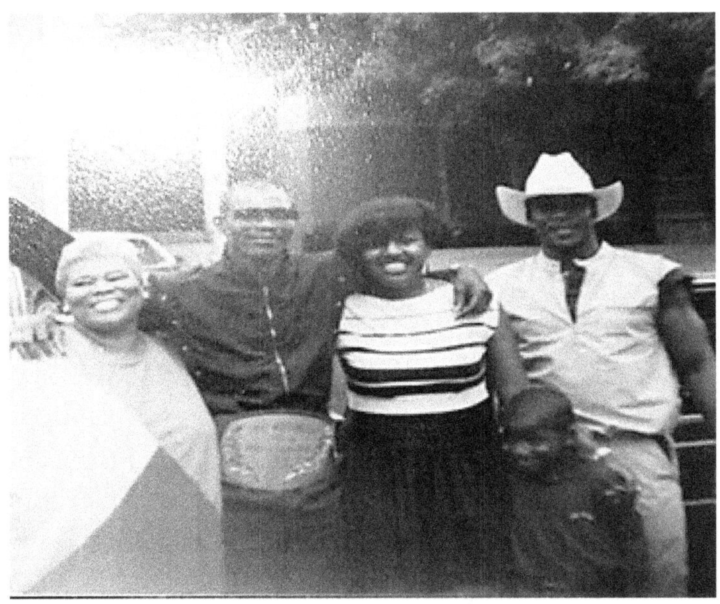

Leroy and neighborhood children

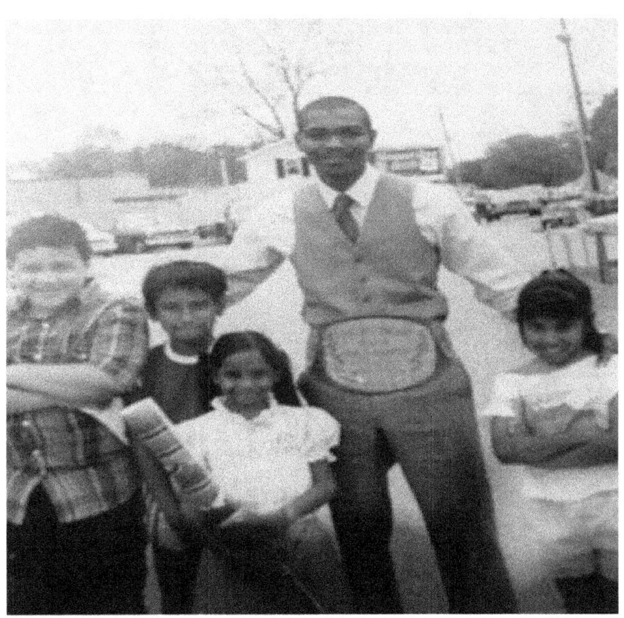

Leroy went on to defend his title against #1 Contender Ismael Robles, in his hometown of El Paso, Texas. Robles was well respected and had said that he would knock Leroy out. Well, the fight did not pan out as he dreamed. He was the one knocked out.

Leroy's next major fight was with the "Golden Boy" Jerry Trimble at Karatemania in the Battle of Atlanta in 1986. This was a huge Triple Championship fight card with Heavyweights' Contender Jerry Rhome vs Heavyweight Champion "Bad" Brad Hefton, Light-Middleweight Champion Bob "Thunder" Thurman vs Middleweight Champion "The Iceman" Jean Yves Theriault, and Light Welterweight Contender Jerry "Golden Boy" Trimble vs Light Welterweight Champion Leroy "Superfeet" Taylor.

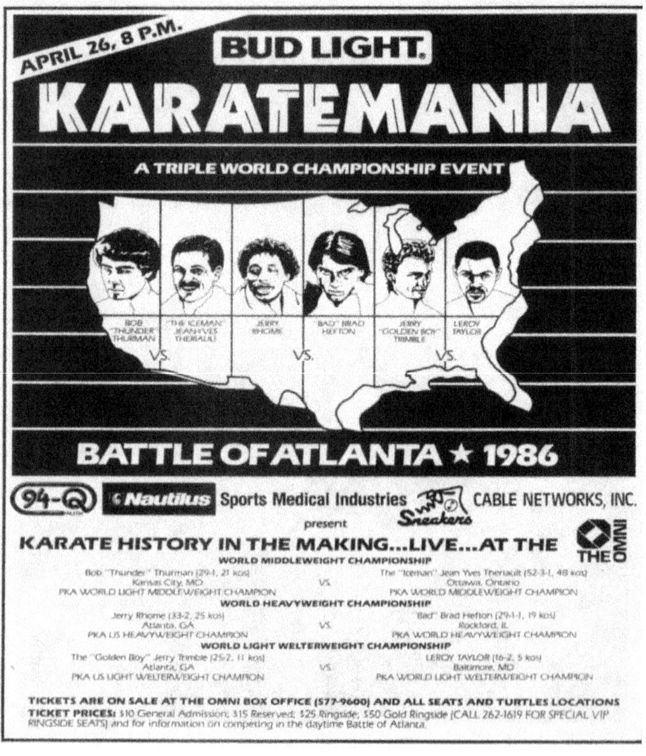

There was a lot of tension in the air and a lot of bad blood that evening. The toughest opponent I ever fought, Bob Thurman, whom I had lost to twice, befriended me that evening and asked me to stay between him and Theriault in the pre-fight ceremonies. I remember thinking: *What am I going to do if they start throwing fists at each other, both of them been knocking everybody out?* So I just stayed clear of them and close to Leroy where I was supposed to be.

Leroy started the fight slowly, which was his usual method. He would pick it up in the later rounds. In the fourth round, Leroy got a bad cut and blood was running in his eye preventing him from seeing. The fight was stopped on what was ruled *an unintentional head butt*. When it went to the scorecards, Trimble was ahead on points and he was declared the new PKA Light-Welterweight World Champion. It was a very emotional time not only for Leroy but for me, his family, his teammates, his karate students, his friends, and the city of Baltimore.

After a couple of months of rest and reconciliation, I consulted with Leroy and Jerry and I informed them that we were re-constructing our training program. From that fight we learned a valuable lesson: *Fights are only one round at a time.* After we got over the shock, I used this unforeseen loss as a training tool and based my decisions on the lessons learned.

I remember Speedo Brown telling me that we probably learn more from losing than we do from winning. I realized that this only occurs when we refocus the hurt, pain, and emotion into positive thinking and evaluation. From that point on, that is how Leroy fought. His re-match with Trimble was again held in Atlanta, Georgia, and, this time. it ended in a draw.

I thought that it was action-packed from beginning to end and Leroy out kicked him. Leroy broke the record for the most kicks ever thrown in a fight with 182 kicks, but it was still not enough to win. He still came up short on the decision; they scored it a DRAW!

We Almost Made It!

Leroy's next fight came after he had been ranked as the PKA and Professional Karate Council (PKC) Number-One Contender. The PKC United States' title had been placed up for grabs and Leroy got the call to fight number-four ranked contender, Ken Comer. Ken Comer was coming off a knockout victory of Leo Loucks, whom Leroy went the distance with for the world title. Ken was pumped with the thought that he could do the same to Leroy.

Leroy went out with bad intentions and after a few rounds of punishing kicks to the body and snapping kicks to the head accompanied by strong hand combinations, Comers was in survival mode. Leroy hurt him several times, but being the competitor and gentleman he is, it appeared he held back from knocking Comer out. He dropped him in the 9th round to seal the victory, sending a message to the other contenders, especially Jerry Tremble. However, for some reason, he never got a third fight with Jerry Tremble.

Leroy lost the PKC U.S. Light Welterweight Title to Ricky Haynes, which turned out to be a weight mismatch. His opponent was a top-ranked Welterweight Contender and outweighed him by at least 20 pounds. The weigh-in was held the day before the fight.

The limitation was supposed to be 143 to 147.9 lbs and Leroy weighed only 143 lbs. His opponent weighed at the top end of the weight limit the day before the fight. By fight time, he had gained most of that weight back and looked like he weighed about 160 lbs plus. This was his natural weight so he was much bigger and stronger.

The fight lasted about nine rounds and Leroy took a terrible beating. I wanted to stop the fight a few times but Leroy wanted to go on. It was not a good night. But nothing could prepare us for the worst that happened a few years later.

Leroy was shot six times while getting food for his grandchildren at a local corner fast-food restaurant. I remember the day that I got the call that Leroy had been shot. My heart dropped as I feared the worst. But God kept him in His arms of protection and allowed him to be a testimony of his grace and mercy.

It was Halloween night after his annual party for the karate children at the Dojo. Sensei was driving his grandchildren home and stopped to get them something to eat. He just happened to stop at a chicken place on North Avenue across the street from the Fire Station. Leroy said he had ordered his food and was on the telephone when a guy came in and started talking to him. He said he told the guy, several times that he was on the phone and he would talk to him later. The guy was persistent, so he just ignored him and kept talking. The guy mumbled something and left the store.

After getting his order, Leroy left the store and a guy put a gun to his head and started talking to him. He told me that the only thing that he could see at that moment was his grandchildren in the car looking at him. At that time, he told me that he said to himself: *I cannot go out like this!* He swept the guy's leg out from under him and he hit the ground. Then the guy shot him in the leg and he went down to the ground.

The guy got up and began shooting him. With each shot, he said it was so painful that he screamed and rolled. The guy shot him six times, amazingly missing any vital organ. Afterward, the guy ran down the street and shot someone else and killed them. Leroy was fortunate that the Fire Station was across the street. The firemen came to his rescue. It was God sending his angels!

Thanks be to God for His grace and mercy, allowing Leroy to survive the near-fatal shooting. He recovered after many months of therapy and rest. He returned to teaching as well as competing locally and nationally.

Each year, Leroy sponsors a karate tournament that many top-ranked local and national practitioners attend. His tournament is geared mainly to children and young practitioners.

Sensei celebrates with students

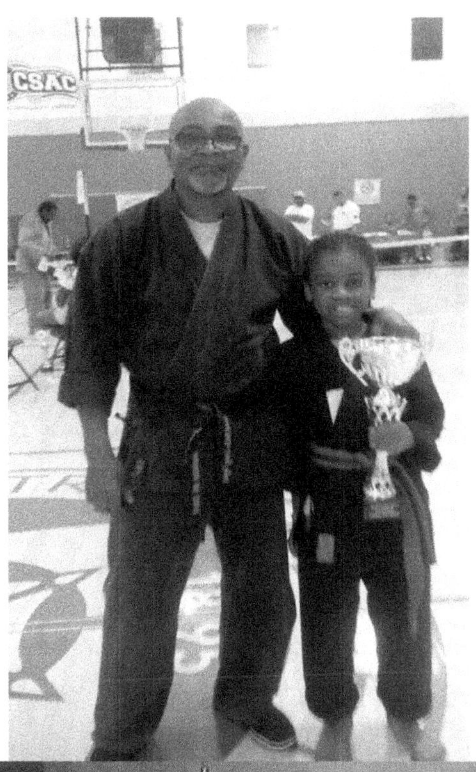

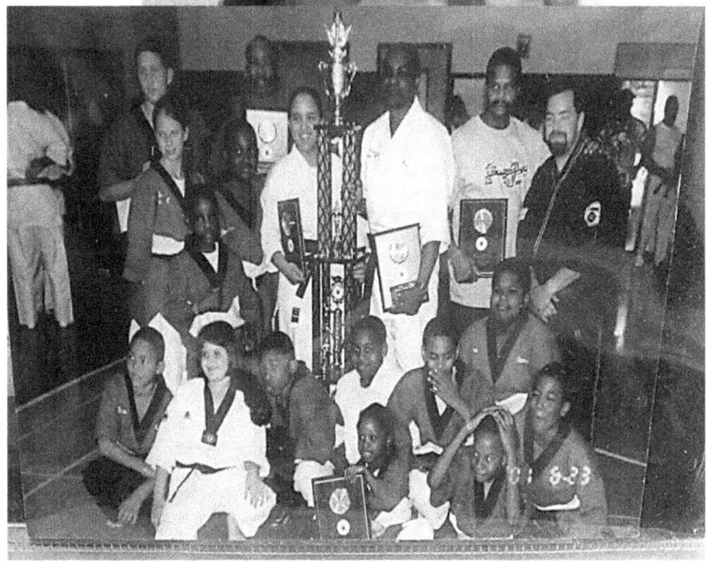

The winning never stops

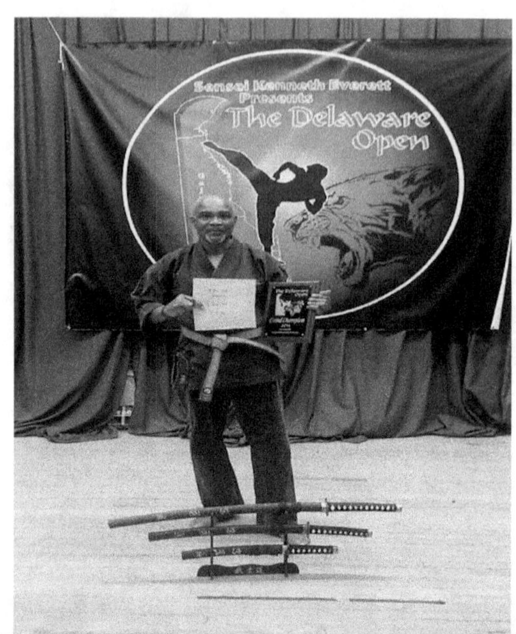

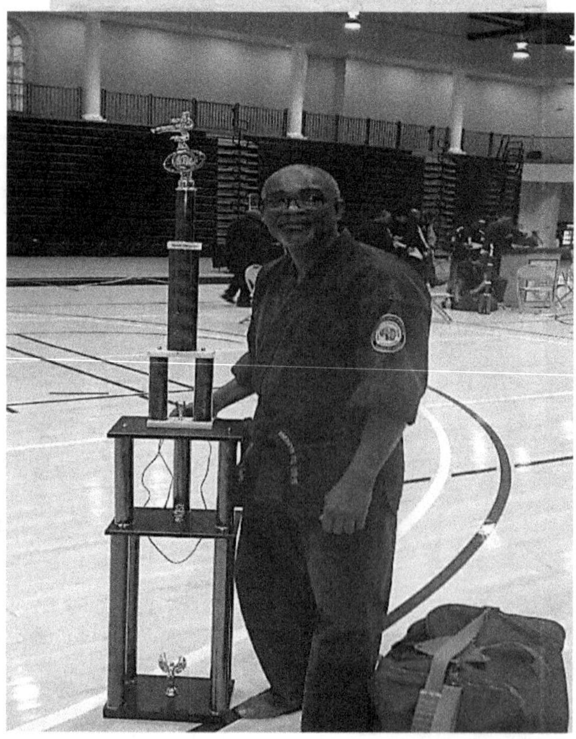

The winning never stops

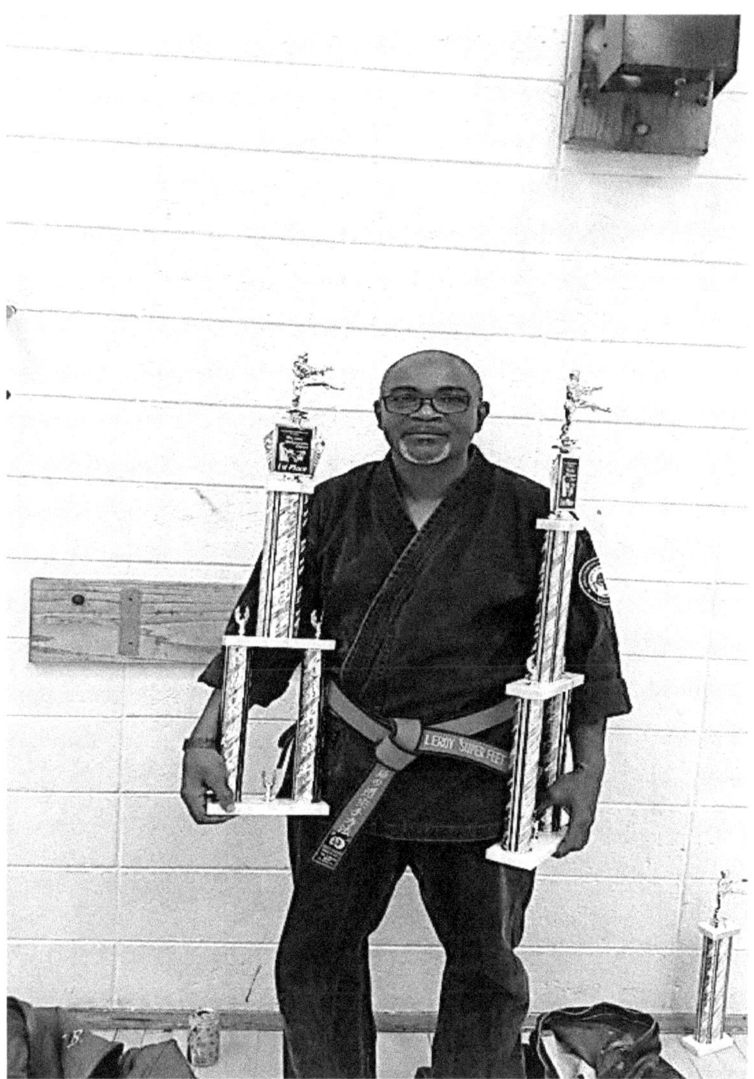

Guest Speaker at the Pentagon

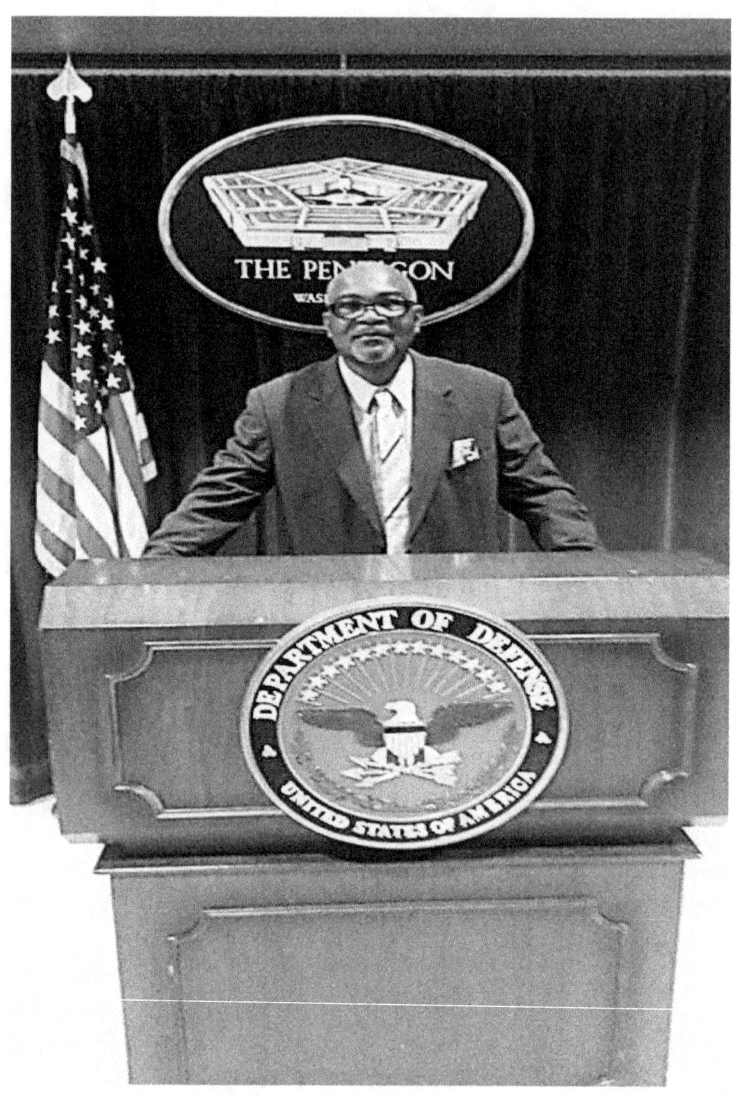

Grand Master Leroy Taylor has been the Head Karate Instructor for over 40 years.

Owner of A-Plus Taylors School of Martial Arts & Fitness in Woodlawn, MD.

Grand Master Taylor's Achievements and Titles Include:

- Professional Full Contact Karate Fight Record 17-4-1

- 3-time World Champion PKA Professional Karate Association Light Welterweight Champion

- PKC Professional Karate Commission Light Welterweight Champion

- FFKA Fight Factory Karate Association Welterweight Champion

In Professional Kickboxing and Tournament Karate:

- 11-time Continuous Contact Champion at the Battle of Baltimore and the Maryland Open Karate Championships

- 2-Time United States Champion

- Fight Factory Karate Association (FFKA) United States Champion

- PKC United States' Champion

- 4-time North American Sport Karate Association (NASKA) Champion

- Professional Karate League (PKL) National Champion

Grand Master Taylor also won a Bronze Medal in 1985 as a member of the U.S. World Kumite Organization (WKO) Karate Team that competed in London England against 30 other countries.

Grand Master Taylor has been invited to speak at several Baltimore City and County elementary, middle, and senior high schools about the importance of a good education and having a healthy mind and body.

Grand Master Taylor is a loving father and devoted husband who continues to teach young people the value of living, loving, and respecting their own family, community, and world at large.

Chapter 2

Sylvester Cash

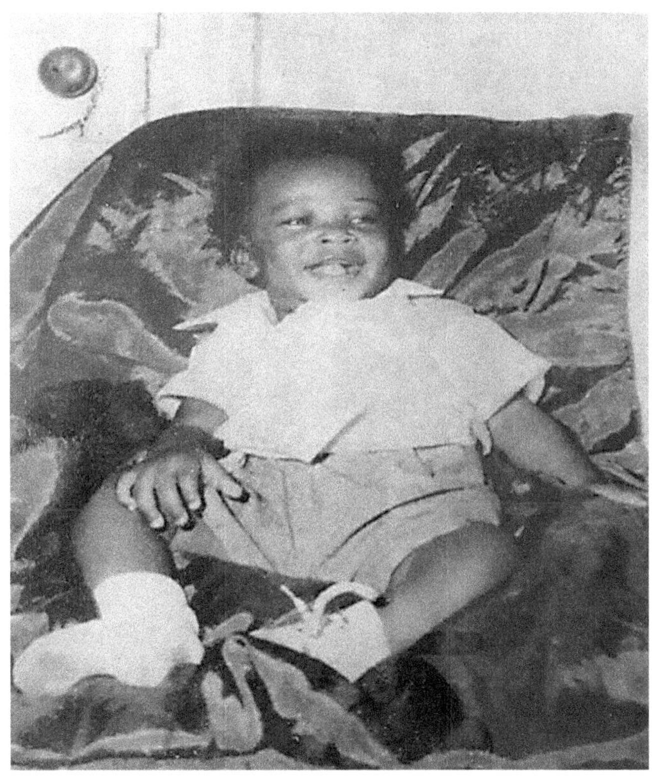

This is one of the harder things that I have had to do for myself in this lifetime and *it ain't over yet*, so I am sure more things are to come. Writing about yourself does not come easy to most of us, especially introverts. We get caught up in what people will think about us:

He is just bragging about himself.

Who really cares what they have done?

I constantly think about what I should say, what I shouldn't say, and the list goes on. So I am starting this way:

Hi. I am Sylvester Cash! I am the first-born of Agnes Pope. I was born on Friday, December 17, 1954, in Baltimore, Maryland at University Hospital. Since I was born on a Friday and my mother was only 17 years old, I probably messed up her whole week.

Family

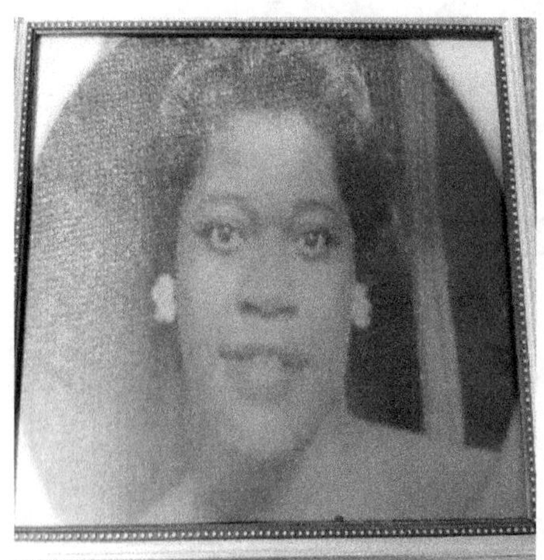

My momma was born on March 13, 1937, in Spring Hope, North Carolina. I was told my Mom was a very strong and determined woman in her younger years. I was told she was a fighter and she backed down from no one. I was unlucky enough to witness a couple of those times in my childhood.

My mom was one of 13 children of Sidney and Henrietta Pope. She grew up on a farm and worked the tobacco and cotton fields of Nash County, North Carolina. She attended Nash County public schools but only completed the ninth grade.

She left the farm before the age of 16 and went north to Baltimore and started a new life and family. It was while living in Baltimore that she met my father, Abraham Cash, and I was conceived.

There were seven of us, five boys and two girls, all by different fathers, I think. We never really talked about our fathers. All of us survived the streets of the ghetto except my youngest brother, Stephen Alexander Wilson, aka *Feedie*. The violence of the streets and drugs ended his young life. I can only imagine that this was one of the lowest, if not the lowest time, of my momma's life because I know it was one of mine!

Before I get into stories about myself, I am going to tell you something about my momma. She worked many jobs to keep us clothed and fed and with a roof over our heads. She even got us on public assistance, which was known as welfare, so that we could have enough money for housing and medical care.

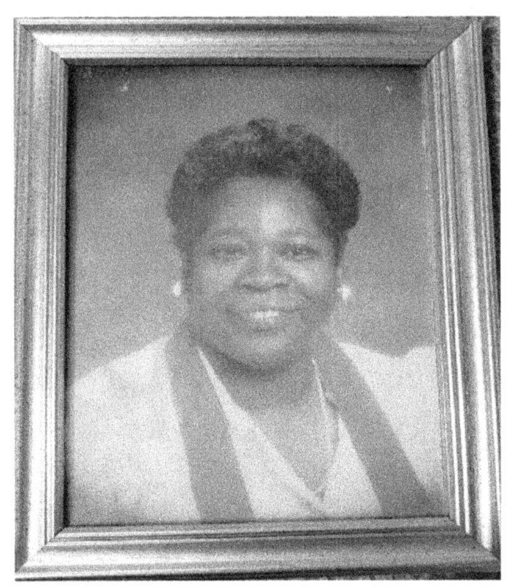

It took many years of struggle, but by the grace and blessing of God, she was able to not only pass the Maryland State GED Program and receive her High School Diploma but to go on and complete her A.A. Degree at the Community College of Baltimore and her B.A. at Coppin State University. She received two degrees in Early Childhood Development.

Because she loved children, my mom dreamed of someday opening her own Daycare Center. I was going to partner with her to help make this dream a reality when illness struck her unexpectedly. She settled with raising and educating her grandchildren.

Momma was a great cook. Her Sunday meals—fried chicken, potato salad, collard greens, cornbread, and the list goes on—were indescribable. Momma could not only cook but she could bake. When she baked cakes, I would just stand there waiting to lick the bowl. When she made banana pudding, everyone would *just happen to stop* by our house for a visit. I think that is where my love for cooking came from. I learned so much from watching her in the kitchen.

I think we never realize our much our mothers really teach about life but take it for granted. I know I did. She taught me how to clean the house, wash, and iron clothes, sew, etcetera, but I just thought she was giving us something to do. I never thought that she was teaching me all this so I could do for my brothers and sisters or take care of myself.

When I think back, I remember her telling me that I should always be able to take care of myself and not have to depend on a woman to do it for me. There were many things over the years that she would tell me, but like most young people, I never really listened or thought about what she was trying to teach me. I am pretty sure it was the same with all of us. We all think back and are remembering and listening now.

Momma finally had enough income coming in and with the help of my sisters and me, to qualify to get in a program for first-time homeownership. She loved her house and finally having a place to call her own. She loved flowers and growing things so one of her first projects was to plant a garden. She had a large backyard so she would have cookouts on holidays and special occasions and she invited everyone.

I have always regretted that I did not have a better relationship with momma, but I am grateful for the years in my adult life when I did get closer to her. She was the one that I found myself going to when I was trying to make decisions about things that I would not go to my friends about.

I remember when I was in the Marine Corps and came home one weekend, I showed her these pipes that I had just brought. I was telling her that I was going to stop smoking and that is why I brought the pipes to help me quit. Well, momma had smoked for over 20 plus years and one day she just stopped. She told me, *if it is something that you don't want to do, you just don't do it.* I heard her loud and clear and, from that moment on, I never smoked again.

I was not the greatest father in the world, but many times momma was there to take up the slack where I was failing. It would have to be something really important before she would call me in to handle it.

When I got custody of my daughter, Shari, she took her into her home because she knew that I was not responsible enough to take care of her. I worked a lot and was still trying to run after the ladies. After Shari was born, I started to bring Myra around to stay with her more.

Then Sylvester Jr. was born and then Kenneth. Except for Myra, all of them were close in age. When all of them would come over, she would put them all in her car and take them everywhere with her, like it was just one. They would go to the green field to pick greens; to the apple orchard to pick apples. She'd take them to the Farmers Market, to the malls, to Kings Dominion, to parks, and anywhere else she had to go. She would just tell them: *Your Daddy gotta work.*

Momma never would say a word to me about being a responsible parent. If there was something that I needed to handle she would call me and say, *You need to come and talk to your young'un.* I knew it was important and went right there. Then, when I would leave, she would call them into her room, especially Shari and Myra, and tell them:

It's alright Baby. Come get in the bed with me.

What he say to you? I'mma get him; it's alright!"

Even though I only talked with them, she would be upset with me for making them cry. She really loved her grandchildren. She would do anything for them.

On October 2nd, the Friday before my wedding, she called all of us together and told us that she was sick. She told us then because she needed a blood transfusion immediately and we needed to be tested to see who was compatible on that Monday.

For about four months, we watched her try to deal with the pain. She would sit and read her bible and pray because she could not lie in her bed anymore. However, she never complained! God finally came and took her home on February 10, 1995.

I was working on my side job when I received a phone call saying that she wanted to see me. She told me she had agreed to go into a Hospice Center, which I thought was just another treatment center. Deep inside I knew she had given up and did not want us to be around her as she made the transition.

I told her was going to close up the house I was working on and I would be right back. Before I reached the house, I received a phone call from the hospital. At that moment, I knew in my heart that she was gone. I continued to the house and closed it up and went back to the hospital where I got the news she had gone home. She never got the chance to see me graduate from Morgan State University that May or become a Mason that April.

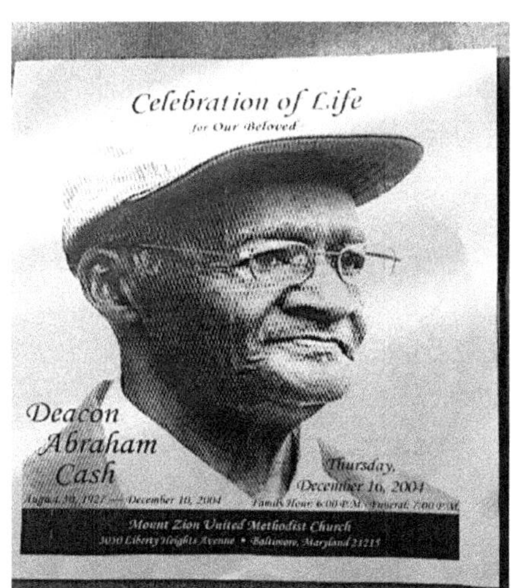

I was given the last name of my father, Abraham Cash. He was born in Stem, North Carolina, on August 30, 1927, and passed on December 10, 2004. He was one of eleven children of Jim and Cora Clark Cash. My Mom was also born in North Carolina, but from what I know, they met in Baltimore. He was a very handsome man. In those days, he was known as a *Lady's Man.*

As I found out years later, my father was a man that did not like confusion. I only got a chance to spend time with him and got to know him after my Mother passed.

Don't get me wrong, I am not saying that she prevented me from seeing him. Our relationship was just not that strong. I would see him from time to time, but not regularly. Most times I would see him at church and gospel shows.

He was a gospel solo singer. He would always pay his respects to the family at funerals by singing a song and bringing sweet potato and coconut custard pies. After eating his pies, you would not want any others. When he sold pies, people would not just buy a slice, they would buy the whole pie.

My father could not read but owned his own taxi cab and could get anywhere around the city of Baltimore and other cities in or out of the East Coast without a map. In those days there was no such thing as a GPS. He was also a deacon in the church and knew the Bible through and through. He once explained to me a gift he had received from God: counting money. When it came to counting money, you could not short-change him.

The more time I spent with him, the more I began to understand myself and why I acted the way I did and still do. Especially when it came to pretty women, avoiding confusion, and not being threatened in times of conflict! Don't get me wrong, being threatened and being scared are two different things that trigger two different reactions.

Grandpa Sidney Pope Sr.

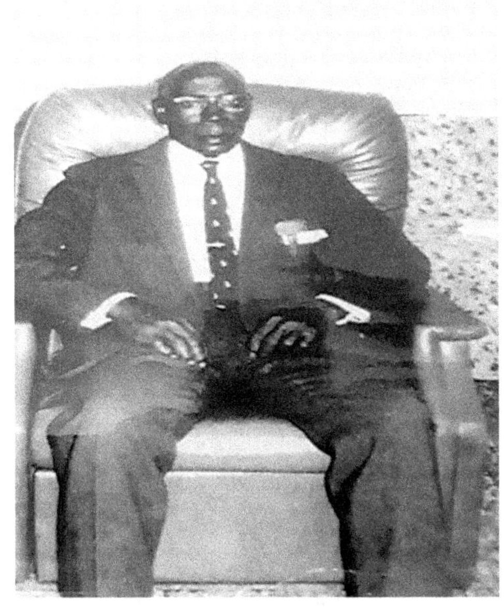

Grand Mother Effie Baines Pope

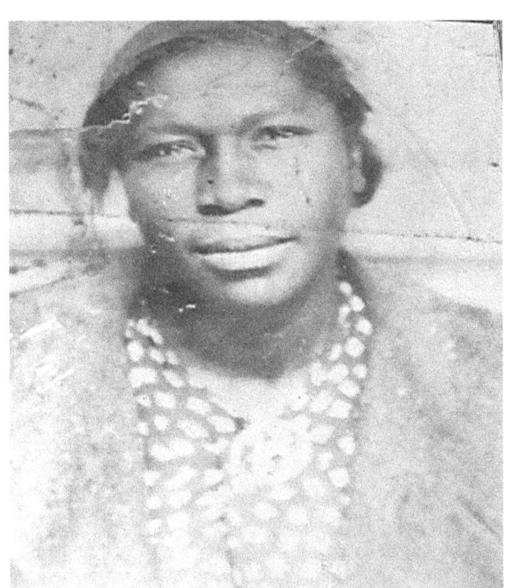

Grand Mother Henrietta Pope

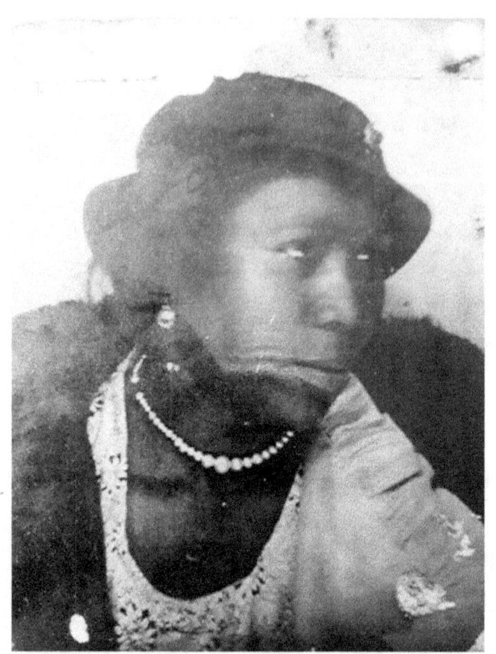

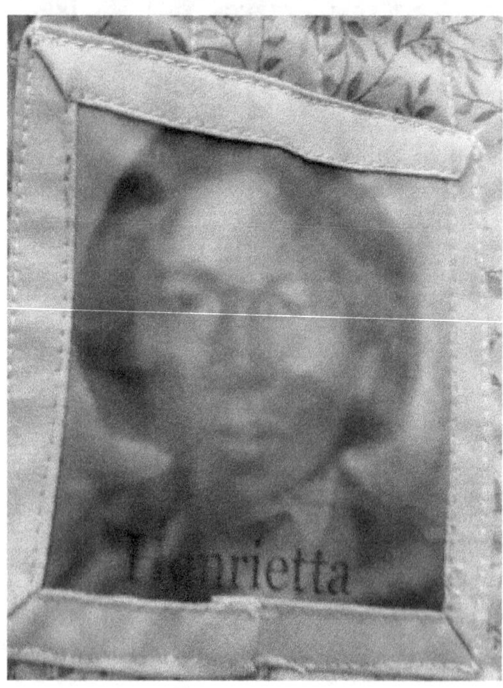

Growing Up

Not to get too deep into my childhood, but I wanted you to have a better idea of what we faced each day living in the ghetto. When I was growing up in the ghettos of Baltimore City, I did not realize how bad I had it.

The reality did not set in until I was an adult and moved out of the country. I think this was mainly because everyone around me lived the same, borrowed from each other, shared clothes with one another, got credit from the same stores, attended the same schools, etc. We knew nothing about what our parents were going through to make ends meet. We knew nothing about what they had to do to keep us clothed and fed, with a roof over our heads.

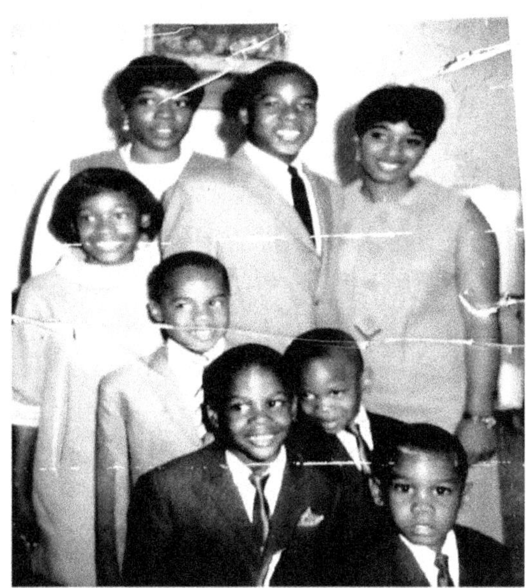

Momma, Me, Mamie, Pam, Anthony, Dennis, Bryan Keith, and Stephen- Easter 1967

I am the oldest of seven: Pamela, Debbie, Anthony, Keith, Dennis, and Stephen. My momma worked two and three jobs cleaning *White/Jewish people's* homes and taking care of their children to take care of us. They called it *day work*, I guess because she would get paid by the day. You needed to know *somebody that knew somebody* to get those jobs.

My momma also received a welfare check each month and welfare rations including powdered milk, welfare cheese, peanut butter, flour, spam, beans, butter, and other items I cannot remember. But I can never forget that welfare cheese. It made the best-grilled cheese sandwiches you ever ate.

Those who were not on welfare would make fun of us, but they would want to borrow some of that welfare cheese. I don't know about my other brothers and sisters, but sometimes things that were said about welfare families really hurt me. Over the years, I learned to ignore it and not let it bring my self-esteem down too far.

My Baltimore city public school system education started at P.S. #142 Elementary School at the age of four years and eight months, because my birthday was in December. Then because we moved, I attended Matthew A. Henson Elementary School #29, Lemmel Junior High School, Carver Vocational Technical High School, and finally graduated from Frederick Douglass Senior High School.

Home

I remember us living on the corner of North Avenue and Smallwood Street, over a store, in an apartment on the 3rd floor. My aunt Gladys lived across the street and I would go to her house after school when Momma was at work. My Momma and her friends would go over there and play cards on Friday and Saturday nights.

Friday and Saturday nights were the best times for us, especially after check day. My cousins Darryl (Puggy), Jerome (Little Bit), and James Jr. (Pee Pee) would come over and stay with us. We would have submarine sandwiches from Sachs Sub Shop. They made the best and juiciest subs in the world! Eating subs and watching TV on Friday and Saturday nights made life great!

My favorite shows were *Honey West, The Wild, Wild West, The Green Hornet, The Adams Family, The Rifleman,* and, when we were brave enough, *The Twilight Zone* and *Alfred Hitchcock.* We would watch TV until it went off at 02:00 a.m. We always hated hearing the *Star-Spangled Banner* play because we knew television was going off and we had to go to bed. We would click through all three channels looking for another movie, but at 02:00, everything went off.

I remember a small fire starting one night, in our third-floor apartment. We all got out safely, but that next week was not so pleasant for this six-year-old. I remember getting ready to leave school and the teacher telling me I could not go home as there had been a fire at my house. She walked me out of school to the corner and I saw that my house had burned down. I went to my Aunt Gladys's house until Momma got home. The good thing was that nobody got hurt. That was the first of a couple of fires that we encountered during my childhood.

After staying with my aunt for a while, we moved to 1540 Payson Street where I attended a small school on Westbury and Payson Streets named #142 Annex. The city was building our new school, Matthew Alexander Henson School #29. The school was being named after the first Black Man to step foot on and explore the North Pole.

Matthew Alexander Henson was born on August 8, 1866, and died on March 9, 1955. His parents' farm was east of the Potomac River in Charles County, Maryland. They were sharecroppers who had been free people of color before the American Civil War.

Matthew's parents were subject to attacks by the Ku Klux Klan and other white supremacist groups that terrorized southern freedmen after the Civil War.

To escape from racial violence in southern Maryland, in 1867, the Henson family sold the farm and moved to Georgetown, then still an independent town part of Maryland and adjacent to the national capital. Mathew Henson spent most of his early life in Washington, D.C., but left school at the age of twelve to work as a cabin boy. He later returned to Washington and worked as a salesclerk at a good department store.

One of his customers was Robert Peary who, in 1887, hired him as a personal valet. Their first Arctic expedition together was in 1891. Afterward, Henson became an American explorer and accompanied Admiral Peary on seven voyages to the Arctic for nearly 23 years as a navigator and craftsman. He became known as Peary's "first man."

Like Peary, Henson studied Inuit survival techniques. He is best known for his participation in the 1908-1909 expedition that they claimed to have reached the geographic North Pole on April 6, 1909. Henson proclaimed that he was the first of their party to reach the pole.

While they were building the school, I remember playing a soldier in the construction site with my friend during the summertime. On the weekends we would build a fort and take turns guarding it. This was a time when we were safe in our neighborhood. We would even have sleepovers in makeshift tents in our backyards as we could not afford real tents. Everybody watched out for every child, not only their own. This was a village and everybody raised you.

At School #29, I went from the third grade to the sixth grade. Because of my teachers Mrs. Woodson and, Mrs. Mapp, I learned valuable lessons about loving and caring about your students. I also learned that you don't hit girls!

One day, Mrs. Woodson sent for my mother to come to the school. She told her that I had hit Barbara White. Well, the full story was never told: Barbara had stabbed me in the wrist with a pencil. Nevertheless, my mother took me home and told me to "TAKE OFF MY CLOTHES!" It was all downhill from there.

My mother pulled out the ironing cord and wore me out. The first thing she would always say was, "TAKE YOUR CLOTHES OFF! I AM NOT BEATING YOUR CLOTHES!" I guess they were *her clothes* since she had bought them for me.

For years to follow, I never put my hands on another girl, but during that time some girls would do things to me. Finally, my mother told me that it did not mean I should stand there and get beat up by girls. I was confused but I eventually figured it out.

After our house caught fire twice, we moved up on Bryant Avenue across the street from Druid Hill Park. I met a new friend and life began! We lived on the second and third floors and I had my own room on the third floor. I could see across most of the city and would sneak out at night. My mother caught me sneaking back in one night but I'll tell you about that later!

Hooking School

After elementary school, I attended Lemmel Junior High School and life really changed. I joined the wrestling team under Coach Powell, then the Gymnastics Team under Mr. Douglass Camper. But in the middle of my first year there, I was introduced to "hooking" school! At this time, education had become unimportant to me.

When I got to Lemmel Junior High School, all of a sudden education did not mean as much to me as having friends. I started cutting classes and then "hooking" school. I wanted to be accepted by the guys so I would follow along. It was great or at least I thought so at the time! We had fun all day—we had girls to entertain us and the excitement of evading the Police and Truancy Officers by hopping trains from one end of the tracks to another section. We thought we were clever, deceiving our parents by pretending we were going to school each day.

The thing that some of us feared the most was not getting caught by the Police or Truancy Officers, but getting caught by our parents, especially our mothers. I especially feared my momma! I feared my Momma so much that I would jokingly tell my friends that if I ever got caught by the Police, do not take me home. Take me straight to jail and do not bother to call my momma. You would think that with this degree of fear I would not do stupid things like this!

Well, everything went great that first year at Lemmel Junior High. My momma did not know about me hooking school and I was passing all my classes. I thought I was home free. So, I thought.

I got caught hooking school on the last day of school. My father, whom I had not seen all year, just happened to know my homeroom teacher, Miss Norris, and just happened to talk to her. Well, now he decided to be a GOOD father and tell momma. Well, all I can say is it was not a good summer for me! When momma found out, it was all over and not pretty! It took me most of the summer to heal from that 'whuppen!

When school started back the next year I went religiously, *for a while*. Unlike some of my friends, I did have enough sense to go to class enough to pass. We would go to the parks or the railroad tracks in the spring when we could not go to somebody's house, and party all day. Ironically, the railroad tracks were right behind the school. If the weather was bad, most of the time I would go to school. I would also never miss school on days that I had gym or any sports practice. In junior high school, I took up wrestling, gymnastics, and karate.

You would have thought that I would have learned my lesson but I didn't. I started hooking school again but not as much as before. I just had too much fun! But I was smart enough to go more and pass my classes.

However, I remember one day it was really cold and we hooked school in somebody's basement. I had gotten a three-quarter-length leather coat for Christmas. We were standing around the furnace trying to get warm and we started smelling this odor, it was my new coat burning from the heat! I don't remember how I explained that one or if I ever let my Momma see the coat in a frontal view.

I was a member of the first class that they had ever graduated from the eighth to the ninth grade in high school. I went to the ninth grade at Carver Vocational Technical High School. In the first year, I studied subjects that were foreign to me, like bricklaying, industrial electronics, painting (which I still hate today), and metal shop. We had to do each one for three months, or one quarter. I had no idea then that these classes would be beneficial to me later in life.

Well, I still hooked school that year, but not as much and I did not get caught. Momma probably knew but just prayed that I did not get into trouble and I would get it together. Thank You, mom!

The next year, I picked bricklaying to be my trade. My instructor was Mr. Watson. He was a big man who never really smiled much, at least at us, but he could lay some bricks. He was a good teacher in the classroom also. He would take the best students, usually the seniors, out on jobs on the weekend and in the summer to earn money and community service hours. Needless to say, I never got to go out on the jobs.

Hooking school carried over even into high school. Well, one day I made the stupidest decision of my young life. I decided that I knew enough and did not need to go to school anymore. So, I decided to quit school in the 11th grade. This occurred in March 1971, when we had only 2 ½ months to the end of the school year. That is how smart I was! I never finished the bricklaying course, but in my mind, I had learned and understood enough to be able to work get a job. Wrong again, it was just the opposite.

I used to tell myself that I would go back to night school or a trade school and finish it. Well, it never happened! So sometime during that summer break, some little voice came to my ear and told me I needed to return to school that fall.

I think that was the beginning of me making smart decisions on my own. Believe you me, I have not made many but I think that was the first and I have never regretted it.

 I am just so happy and blessed that my momma had enough confidence in me to not say a word that whole summer. She just let me figure it out for myself. All I remember her saying to me was: "I just want you to know, your sisters and brothers are watching you. You are setting a good example." That statement was one of the most productive things momma ever said to me. It always stuck with me. If nothing else, I love my sisters and brothers and there was nothing I would not do for them. So, I have always been careful not to embarrass them by my actions.

Now, I realize that it had to be rough for my momma and I know I worried her tremendously. As children growing up, we never, ever thought or cared about what we were putting our parents through; it was all about us. But that type of pain and worrying goes beyond our immediate family to all those that live under the same roof as well as to our extended family: our grandparents, aunts, uncles, cousins, and their friends. I believe it now when they say: "It takes a village to raise a child." We are not in this thing called life alone!

Going back to school put me around winners and positive people. I am not saying that I was not already around that caliber of people, but I just never realized it or looked at them that way. I was associated with being on a winning football and track team. In the following years, being a winner and a finisher became my way of life and thinking for me.

The choices we make in life!

Sometimes, as we get older, we begin to question the choices that we have made in life. We start to rethink and evaluate why we made those choices. We try to form some type of rationale for the way things turned out. How did we get here?

The people I have met, and those who have forgotten they ever knew me, probably still have no idea what I have done in my lifetime. Most don't know my accomplishments in work and play; the setbacks I have experienced; the people I met on the journey; the good choices and the not-so-good choices I made in my lifetime.

Looking at the smile I try to wear on my face, they don't have any idea of the pain I endured and that I still endure. They don't know the rough roads and deep valleys that I have traveled or the paths I am still traveling.

I guess being an introvert has helped me to conceal a lot of things in my life like feelings and emotions. There is a saying, "People will not know how ignorant you are until you open your mouth." I guess I have subconsciously used silence to hide and endure my pains and insecurities. As I have gotten older and more confident in myself, I have loosened this defense mechanism. I have shared some of these things with only a few close friends and people that I thought my painful and heartfelt experiences would help.

I have shared these stories with some that thought they had come to the end of their journey and could not see past the dark clouds of the night. I let them know that my life has not been all that easy and comfortable either. I try to show them that if God would save me, then he would also save them. I also remind them, as I reflect on the lyrics of an old spiritual song: "Nobody told me that the road would be easy. I don't believe he brought me this far to leave me."

We all have experienced hardships of some form or another, especially the ones that are similar to those I am about to share with you. Through it all, they have made us stronger and wiser. What my hardships show are the blessings and comforts that I have received from my God's grace. Every moment of our lives, He gives us and surrounds us with His grace and blessings. The Bible teaches us that "His grace is sufficient."

Well, as I stated before, I am the oldest of seven children. When I was growing up in the ghettos of Baltimore, I never really thought about how my decisions, good or bad, would affect my entire life to come. The reality that my decisions had consequences did not come to light until I became a more seasoned, responsible adult with my own children and started working with youth. We could have never contemplated what our parents were going through to make ends meet or what they had to do to keep us clothed and fed with a roof over our heads.

As I stated earlier, after elementary school I attended Lemmel Junior High School and my life really changed. My focus became on friendship and good times and not on education. I think that this was the start of my bad decision-making. This behavior eventually caused me to make one of the stupidest decisions of my life—quitting school in the 11th grade near the end of the school year. Yes, that's right, I dropped out of school.

I sat around the house every day watching television for the next couple of months. I contributed nothing to the family, especially to my younger brothers and sisters. I was on the path to a wasted life.

I got to know all the shows by heart and I could tell what time it was by what show was on. Momma would still go to work, as usual, and say nothing to me about school. Some nights she would come and ask me to help her with her math homework. She was also taking classes to help her prepare to take the GED exam.

I remember her only saying to me once, "Your brothers and sisters are watching you." Those words hit home and dug deep inside of me! Especially after she had completed the very challenging GED exams and showed me the results. Her highest score was in math. I remember thinking to myself, "Something is wrong with this picture!"

As a result of my dropping out, I missed out on the opportunity to learn the bricklaying trade that would have gotten me connected with the trade unions and good jobs.

 I finally got my head back on straight that summer and went back to school. I was accepted into Frederick Douglass Senior High School, which happened to be my former high school rival. When I first got there, the principal, Mrs. Edna Campbell, met with me and momma. Mrs. Campbell was a short, slightly gray-headed, no-nonsense woman. She told me straight out that if I screwed up in any way, she would kick me out. And I believed her!

When I got there, I joined the Junior Varsity Football team. I played guard on offense. The reason I got that position was one of the guys, Cleveland, who became one of my best friends, offered to let me play the position of the offensive guard. I was not that big, but I was strong and fast. I later would alternate as the full-back. At that position, I earned the name "truck" because I would just run over everybody.

After the winter season was over, I ran track. I ran the high and low hurdles, ran the 220 dash, the relay teams, and threw the shot put. Because I was in gymnastics, I long jumped and became a pole vaulter. I was very versatile.

In my senior year, I earned a spot on the Varsity Track team. I had some of the top runners in the state in my school: Daniel Lund, Clifford Wiley, and Rickey Moore. Then there was middle-distance runner Derrick McCulloh, whom I had known from childhood when I was in the Cub Scouts. His Mom, Mrs. McCulloh, was our Den Mother.

Clifford Wiley made the United States 1980 Summer Olympic team for the 400 meters, but the U.S. boycotted the Moscow Olympics. Rickey Moore went on to play professional football for the Indianapolis Colts and the Green Bay Packers. I lost track of some of the others. It was off to the Marine Corps for me!

But, thankfully, through the grace of God, momma, and other family and friends' prayers, I finally began making smarter decisions, which I have never regretted! As a result of these positive and productive decisions, I was also able to go on to college and earn a B.S. Degree in Business Management and a Master's Degree in Public Administration. This enabled me to be eligible to attend the Federal Law Enforcement Academy and enter a four-year Plumbing Apprenticeship program.

Childhood Friends

Bryant Avenue was a great neighborhood to live in. People were friendly, many kids were around the same age, and we walked to school together.

My first friend was Delonzo Jiggetts. Delonzo lived up the street from me and went to Lemmel also. He had two brothers—Cedrick (Armas) and Theodore. His mother, Ms.

Dorothy, was a tailor/seamstress, very outspoken, and she could back it up! She took me in as one of her sons.

Then there was Auntie (Mrs. Parker); Pop (their grandfather, Mr. Jiggetts); Alfred (a friend living there); and the cousins (the Parkers): Barbara, Lester Jr., Baba (Reginald), and Donnie.

I had another good friend there, Carroll Parker. He lived on the third floor on the corner of Auchentroly Terrace, just him and his Mom. As the years went on, friends grew and life began. If I can, I'll find a way to mention all of those that I can still remember and apologize to those that I have forgotten or neglected to mention. There are so many whose faces I can see but whose names elude me.

The friends I remember the most are Charles Wheatley, Kenny Johnson, Sidney (Philip) and Gerald Johnson, Michael Gilford and his brother Larry, Gary and Bobby Taylor, Marvin Murphy, Larry, and George Harriston.

I also remember Joe, Gaggie and Lenny Jenkins, JW and Tyrone, Charles Wheatley, Kenny and Bobby Johnson, Donald and CJ Johnson, Bo, Maynard, Ralph Jefferson, Quincy Speaks, Lepp, Rayford Perry (Penn), JW and Tyrone Bailey, Glenn and Bobby Lee, Myron, Quinton, and Mr. Charles Johnston.

As I said, we had a lot of talent and characters in my neighborhood. All of my friends had some unique ways that would sometimes put us in tears with laughter. We had wannabe players, athletes, entertainers, and future potential geniuses. My friends would give us nicknames for things that we did that were either amazing, stupid, or by our personality. My family called me *Snook*. I never knew why, but my friends changed it to *Snooky* which I liked better.

Some years later I found that my aunt Leila Royster, my father's sister, was named *Snook* also. I don't know what it was with them to give the same name to other family members. I also found that I have a cousin, on my father's side, named Sylvester Alexander Cash, a great guy. So, I know there are at least three Sylvester Cashes in this world.

I was very strong and solid growing up. One day, I got into a fight with some guy passing through the neighborhood, and he attempted to stab me in my leg with a folding knife. When the knife hit my leg, it folded back in and fell apart, so they started calling me "Superman."

When we played football, we played with no protective equipment and I would take all kinds of hits and just keep going. We played football anywhere: on the concrete sidewalk or in the street with the cars parked on the sides. Once I ran into one of those old cars when cars were made of steel. I was running out for a pass and when I turned back around it was lights out, I had run into the car and knocked myself out. The guys brought me to and we continued to play.

Another time we were playing football in the park, Armas and I were going to tackle Tony Dennis. He was supposed to hit him high and I was going to tackle him low. Well, we both went low. We missed Tony and I hit his head with my mouth. I bent my upper front teeth backward in my mouth. I grabbed them with my fingers and straightened them back up before going home. Momma, while fussing at me, took me to the hospital and they stitched up my lip and gum where the upper part of my teeth had penetrated and sent me home. They told me to come back on Monday when the dentist would be in. This was the first time that I ever remember going to the dentist.

In those couple of days, my mouth got infected from not being properly treated. For the next six months, I got needles in my mouth every Monday. The last needle I got was the one that brought tears to my eyes. I was afraid of needles from that point on. I was fortunate only to lose one of my front teeth after I got older.

Even after all that I still loved to play football. I still played in the street, on concrete, on lots, on the grass, or any other place we could play. I played my first organized football with a team we named the "Westside Evergreen." I do not know how we came up with that name, but it was what it was.

Our coaches were men that volunteered their time and knowledge to help us. I think they were friends of Mr. Charles. They got us uniforms and pads and they also provided transportation to our games outside of our neighborhood.

The one person that I really remember was Coach Brown, who we called Fire Chief because he was a Fireman. He was a very mild-mannered man. However, we once saw him lose his temper with one of the other coaches who were twice his size. He wrestled him down to the ground in no time and it was over.

I played guard and running back because I was strong and fast. That was the only season I played because I went to high school the following year. We had a great season and I learned a lot. In high school, I also played guard and ran fullback. I played against some of my former teammates in high school and we had a lot of fun hitting each other. Because I was so strong, I did not rely on my speed as before. I wouldn't just run around people; I would just run them over.

However, during one game the running over of my opponents turned against me. I was running for the goal line and the free safety was the last person between me and the goal. Instead of trying to run around him, you guessed it, I decided to just run over him. I don't know what he hit me with, but I woke up on the sideline. That definitely knocked some sense into my head that day. I learned to use the pads and not just brute strength, but a little footwork too.

When I started fighting in full contact karate, I picked up another nickname "Ironman" from my Trainer and Head Sensei, Greg "Speedo" Brown. However, that's a story for another time.

One of my best friends was called Penn. I don't know why they called him that, but his name was Rayford Perry. He was a country boy, straight off the farm in South Carolina. He came to stay with his Aunt Ms. Bell and Patricia. Word had it that Patricia was his sister. I never asked and we never talked about it, because it never mattered to me.

He had this country accent, a country smile, and country slang that would make you just break out laughing. One thing about Penn was he could get the ladies. I don't know what he said to them but he had them, especially the homely ones that nobody would go after. He was a couple of years older than me. I never really knew his age or asked. He went to the same junior and senior high schools I went to, but a couple of years before me. He was an excellent swimmer, ran cross country, and played football. He was the punter on the football team. I remember during one game he went to punt the ball and it just went straight up and came straight back down. It was so funny we laughed for days.

After high school, he went into the Army and served in Vietnam. Penn was a real kind-hearted guy. We used to talk about a lot of stuff. When I was going to my Senior Prom, I could not afford to rent a limo to go, so Momma let him use her old, white 1966 Chrysler 300 to drive me to the prom. I did not worry too much about it because I had no date anyway.

Penn was also good with his hands and, being from the country, he knew a lot about cars. After he got out of the Army, he landed a few jobs as a mechanic and eventually as a toll facility policeman. He loved to go out and party and meet new women. One weekend he came home married. The marriage did not last very long. He suddenly found himself in a financial bind, so I moved in with him for a short time to help with the rent.

Penn was not a very good cook. I remember one time he was cooking some fish and potatoes. I told him that if he put the potatoes in the fish grease that they would clean the grease and he could use it for other things to cook. Well, a little while later he called me in to eat. He had cooked some steak fish, but it was still white and he had put a whole potato in the pan of grease and had it just sitting there. I asked him why he had not cut it up and cooked it. He told me, "You didn't say you had to cook it; just put it in the grease." We rolled laughing!

For some reason, Penn took his own life! I never found out why. Some say he had started getting high on cocaine. His weakness was women, and there was a rumor that he hadn't been able to take the loss of another woman. Another said he had lost his job. Whatever happened sent him over the edge, and he committed suicide.

Another character in our clan was Larry Hairston. Larry was a very intelligent brother who just liked to clown sometimes. His uncle was the world-famous comedian, Slappy White. Slappy White and another world-famous comedian, Red Fox, used to come to visit them from time to time. Larry was a tough short guy too. He would not back down from anyone and would always crack a joke to try and diffuse the situation. He was good at football, but would not go out for teams in school.

He loved to tell jokes and make people laugh and he was good at it! When it was warm outside, we would sit on the corners and tell jokes, while some of the other guys would be singing. We would get the older guys to cop us some wine and beer and the night's fun would begin.

Sometimes we would spend all day bumming money to have spending money for the night. One day, we spent all day just asking people walking through the neighborhood for pennies. They would try to give us nickels, dimes, and quarters, but we wouldn't take them, only pennies. Larry would start making a joke of them until they complied. We bummed about twenty dollars in change that day and had a lot of fun doing it! Larry was hilarious!

One spring night, we were sitting out on the steps all up and down Orem Avenue and someone shouted down the street that Larry was being jumped by some guys by the liquor store. A number of us ran up to the corner and Larry and Kenny were fighting four other guys. It became chaotic and when the police came and broke everything up, one guy was dead from being stabbed. Larry was taken to jail and then released. No charges were ever filed and we never found out who stabbed him. After high school, Larry enlisted into the Marine Corps Reserve.

Mr. Charles lived next to our friends Penn and Patricia on Gwynn Falls Parkway. He was an ex-Force Recon Marine and would tell us stories about his time in Vietnam, and also about Malcolm X. Mr. Charles was a nice man, easy to talk to, and cared about us. He would teach us karate and judo and take us out to the park at night and teach us how to ambush the enemy. We really did not understand why, but we enjoyed it.

Because of him, all I wanted to be after that was a Marine. I remember telling him that I wanted to learn to beat the guys up at the bars and parties. He said to me, "If you don't go to those places, you won't have to defend yourself against them." At that point, I started understanding what he was saying and stop doing some of the things I was doing to get into fights.

I remember Mr. Charles started working as a bus driver for MTA. After that, things changed for us. First, he got married! He then moved away and I never saw him again. I still sometimes think about him and how he influenced my life. I just want to tell him THANKS!

Music in the Hood

During the time I was growing up, music was very important in our lives. Back then, songs had meaning. They expressed the community's feelings about love, relationships, political policies, the war in Vietnam, life, and what to expect. We had talent shows that allowed us to compete for prizes and bragging rights in our neighborhoods. We put a lot of pride and time into singing. Singing gave us hope! Hope that we would become big stars and be able to move out of the ghetto and make a lot of money. It also channeled our energy into more positive things. It kept us out of mischief which could have led to more serious trouble.

During the summer, Operation Champ would sponsor mini-concerts in the evenings at different locations in the inner city. They had a large truck that converted into a stage. Most of the popular singing groups in the city would perform.

There were a lot of local Baltimore -groups in the 1960-80s. The top ones were The Whatnauts, Frankie and the Spindles, The Softones, and Dru Hill. Before them were the Swallows with Eddie Rich and Money Johnson, who I got to know personally. I dated one of Mr. Eddie's daughters. They would tell us many stories about their younger days and sing some of their songs, especially during times of socializing.

Many groups originated in Baltimore, but they did not emerge nationally until they moved their acts to Philadelphia. These include such groups as The Flamingos, Ink Spots, The Orioles, The Swallows, The Swan Silver Tones, Soul Stirrers, The Ravens, and The Pilgrim Travelers.

In our neighborhood, we had only a few want-to-be singing groups. We had the street corner singers in every block that had a bar. These were older guys who had washed out in sports or dropped out of school. They would get a bottle of Thunderbird or some Wild Irish Rose Wine with a couple of forty-ounce beers and sing until the bars and cut rates closed. Nobody bothered them except for the police when somebody complained. The songs that they sang were usually about life. There was a story being told and it came straight from the heart.

The Tone Expressions

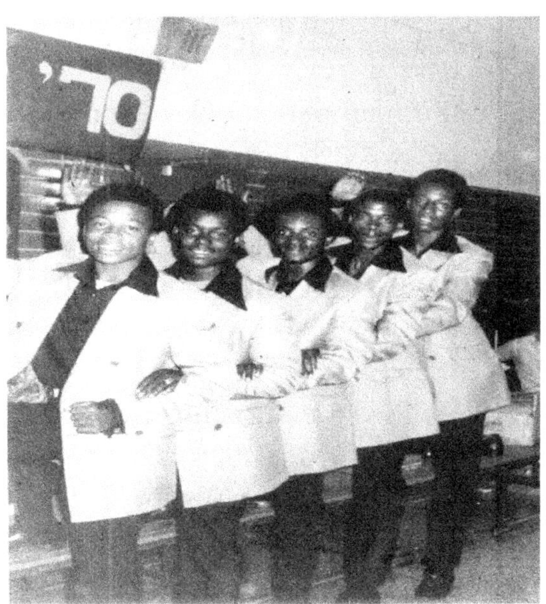

We had the Tone Expressions and the Self Expressions, which I was a member of. The Tone Expressions was made up of a group of guys that came together through one means or another. It was either school or hooking school, sports, parties, or chasing ladies. Bill (Bill Basfield); Sidney (Phillip Johnson); Moe (Garrett Keane), who loved the Temptations, especially David Ruffian; Ronnie (Ronnie Green), who was very quiet (I am not quite sure how he got with them; and Butch (Jeffery Quick), a great guy who loved the ladies as did the rest, loved to dress nice, was a good street fighter. These guys were energetic and pulled it together.

In my opinion, Bill was the most talented. He was a first tenor and could hit all the high notes. WOW! I was always amazed when he hit those notes. I would go somewhere in private and try to hit them. I would have a couple of drinks and try again. The alcohol served two purposes: first, it took away the shyness, and next, it made me think I was hitting the first tenor notes. Sidney, a second tenor I think, could sing all the Intruders' material.

Some of his family members, uncles Money Johnson and Eddie Rich along with his cousin, David Banks were professional singers. David loved the Intruders. Moe, a second tenor, loved the Temptations. He always wanted to sing Dave Ruffin's parts. Ronnie was quiet; I'm not sure what his range was. Butch who was tall, was the bass.

To become known in the entertainment world you needed to know somebody or you need to get discovered. In Baltimore, we had the world-famous Royal Theater and that was the place where people were discovered.

The Royal Theatre was located at 1329 Pennsylvania Avenue and was first opened in 1922 as the black-owned Douglass Theatre. It was the most famous theatre for black entertainment in big cities. All of the biggest stars in black entertainment, including those in jazz and blues, debuted there included:

- Cab Calloway
- Ethel Waters
- Pearl Bailey
- Louis Armstrong
- Fats Waller
- Louis Jordan
- Duke Ellington
- Etta James
- Nat King Cole
- The Platters
- The Temptations
- The Supremes
- Count Basie

All were performers at the Royal. The Royal frequently held shows for local talent. The Tone Expressions worked hard to prepare for this talent show and it paid off. They won a couple of talent shows by singing the song that I loved to hear them sing, *There's a Beauty* by Frankie and the Spindles, another talented local group. They were never able to venture beyond the limits of the Baltimore-Washington Corridor. Tragedy struck the group when Butch Quick was killed. I don't remember the circumstances, but it was said his girlfriend stabbed him.

There was also my group, The Self Expressions, or should I say the-want-to-be Tone Expressions? We were led by one of my best friends, our lead singer Charles Wheatley. Charles was a baritone and could also sing tenor. Bo was our bass, Arthur Glover our baritone, and me the 2nd tenor.

I think that I was only there because Charles and I were best friends and I was also good friends with everyone in The Tone Expressions. Hey, don't get me wrong, I could carry a little bit of a tune or at least make a *joyful noise*. I was good in the background.

The Tone Expressions would tutor us while making fun of us. In time, they recruited Charles into their group. We only did very few shows in Annapolis; no well-known places. But we had fun trying and we loved each other.

Charles Wheatley, Cash, Kenny Johnson 1971

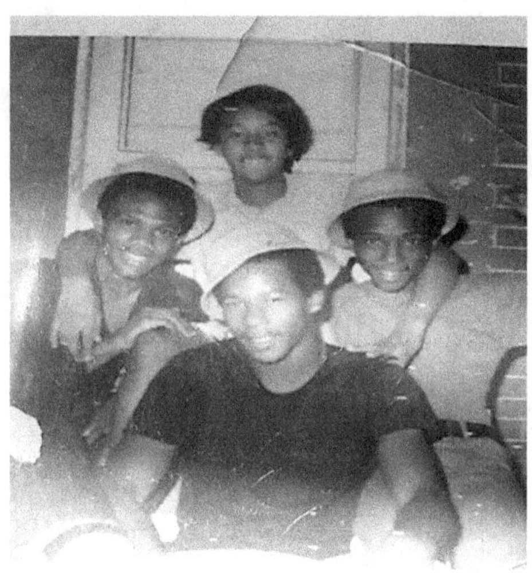

The Ghetto

The ghetto, as defined by Merriam-Webster's Collegiate Dictionary, is *a quarter of the city in which members of a minority group live especially because of social, legal, or economic pressure. A situation that resembles a ghetto conferring inferior status or limiting opportunity.*[1]

Most of us who grew up in the ghetto would say that the definition was a very mild way to describe it! When I use the word *ghetto*, I am talking about the physical and mental conditions of my surroundings. It takes me back to living in poverty. It reminds me of the mental suffering and anguish I endured and the social injustices I experienced. Along with this negative side is also a positive side.

When I think of the ghetto, I also go back to a place where I was more happy than sad. A place where I was safer in the neighborhood than in rural areas. I had more real friends than enemies in the ghetto. I reflect on the times when neighbors helped each other rather than turning their backs and when every adult was your parent and kept watch over you.

In the ghetto, most of us learned survival skills. We learned to be dependent on ourselves and also how to look out for our family members and friends. Surely, not everyone that grew up in the ghetto was a model citizen, but there were more that were than those who were not!

The lessons that I learned while growing up in the ghetto have helped to shape and mold me as the man that I am today. The people that I grew up with and the people I met along the way helped to direct my steps along my journey. My Momma and my immediate family loved me so much

---

[1] Ghetto. 2020. In Merriam-Webster.com. Retrieved August 29, 2020, from https://www.merriam-webster.com/dictionary/ghetto.

that they never made me feel or realize that I was even in a ghetto.

It was not until I was in the Marine Corps that I even realized that I was a "kid from the ghetto" and not a "ghetto kid". They are two different things. My definition may differ from everybody else's definition. Here it is:

A kid from the ghetto is one that grew up in the poor conditions of the inner city. They survived the environment and consequences of poverty — violence, drugs, physical and mental abuse, crime, hunger, neglect, and prejudice. They were able to use the knowledge acquired from everything thrown at them to become upstanding and productive citizens.

Ghetto kids, on the other hand, are on the extreme opposite end of the spectrum.

They are said to be from low-income families and neighborhoods. They dress in all big clothes and can't say words correctly. Even though some are White, they are said to usually be Black. Ghetto kids make fun of people to cover up their insecurities. They have hardly any morals, because they may have experienced or come out of bad family situations.

They may leave the ghetto, but they did not learn to value life, respect others, or other people's property. They are the ones that come into events whether public or private, invited or uninvited, using vulgar language, being disrespectful, and acting like they have no home or social training. They try to eat or drink up everything and, afterward, they try to take plates of food out with them "to feed an army" when they have contributed absolutely NOTHING! I almost became one of them. But, once again, I remembered how I was raised and did not want to embarrass or disgrace my family's name.

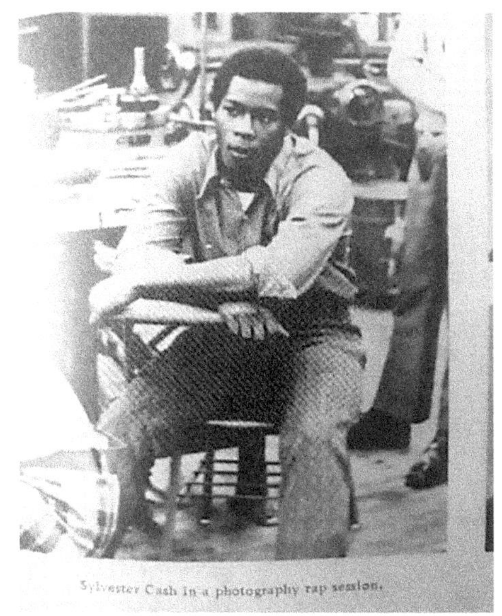

Sylvester Cash in a photography rap session.

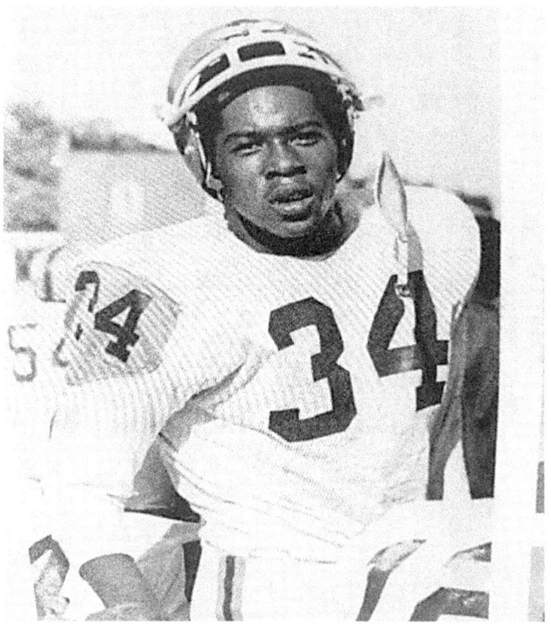

Winning Varsity Football Team 1972-73

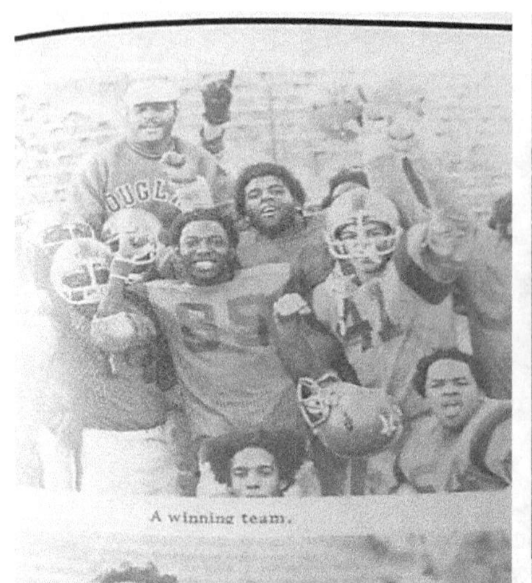

A winning team.

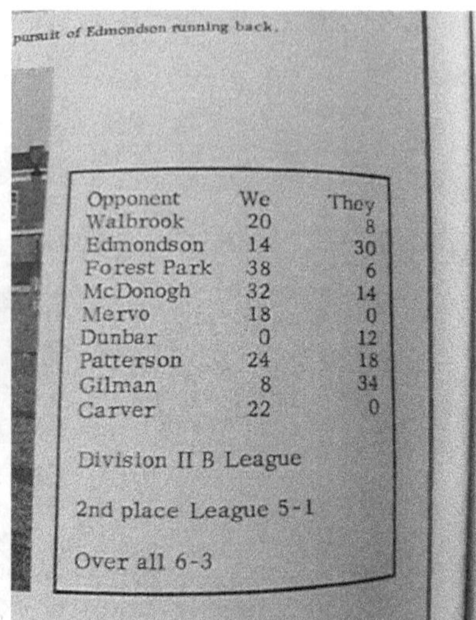

pursuit of Edmondson running back.

Opponent	We	They
Walbrook	20	8
Edmondson	14	30
Forest Park	38	6
McDonogh	32	14
Mervo	18	0
Dunbar	0	12
Patterson	24	18
Gilman	8	34
Carver	22	0

Division II B League

2nd place League 5-1

Over all 6-3

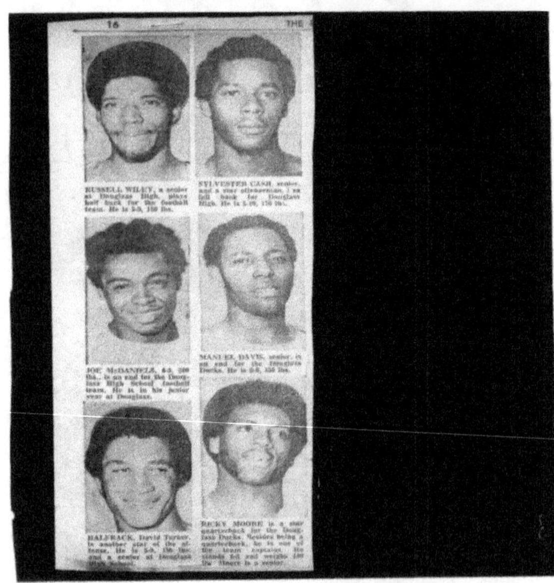

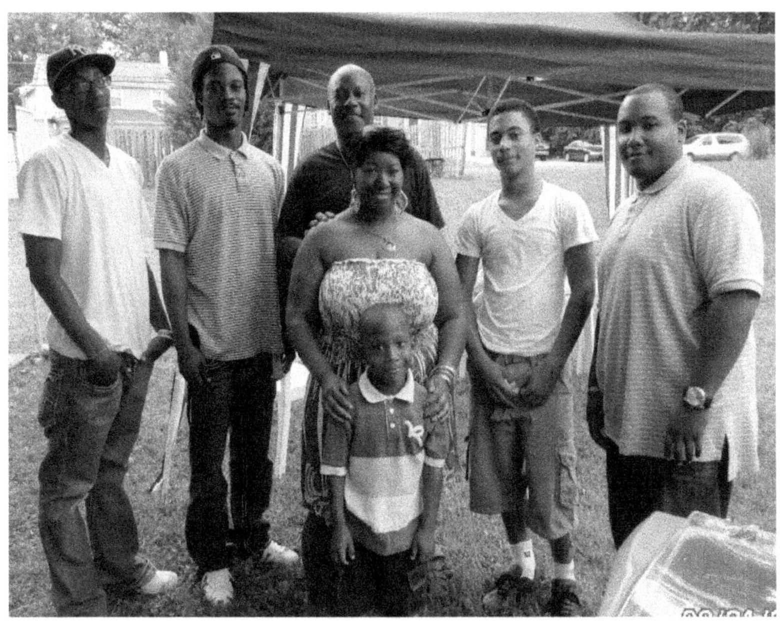

Looking at a different part of life, one of the more important decisions I made coming into mid-life was getting married. I made that decision for what I thought was the right reason: setting a good example for my children, especially my sons. But after three days, I knew it was not going to work.

I know some of you are saying, "Three Days?" Yes, three days. After three days, I saw a big change in her. Where before it was "we and ours," all I heard from then on was "I and mine." I think the big turning point came when I was told that my other children could not come and stay at the house when I was not home. That being said, I could understand why she would say something like that, especially since she had been a single parent.

I worked a lot. I had a mortgage. I paid half of the expenses at the house we were renting, two timeshares—one she insisted we buy—and two car notes. Then Momma was sick and not working and my youngest daughter Shari stayed with her, so I helped pay her household expenses.

I worked my full-time job, for which I was on 24-hour call, and I worked part-time doing my plumbing and security work on the side. I was an active member of the Masons and on the Board of Trustees and chorus at my church. Oh, I also taught karate and women's self-defense at the recreation center and my kickboxing schools.

I was also Mister Mom in the evenings because my wife worked from 3 p.m. until 11 p.m. Even though I had all those other jobs and activities, I was able to attend the school PTA meetings, the kids' programs, and help them with their homework and school projects. On Saturdays, I would take them with me on plumbing jobs so they could see what I did, learn about the trade, and earn a little money. After we finished, I would drive past one of the fast-food places and tell them how much more they had earned in a couple of hours. They were with me and made more than the workers there made in a week. I was trying to give them alternatives.

When I was doing security at Chuckie Cheese, they would have the time of their lives, playing games and eating pizza. And of the night I would show them how much I made for the one night, as compared to those that did not have the credentials and training I had.

Even though the marriage did not work for me, it taught me a few valuable lessons. This list may not be in an order of importance, but in my mind, they are all important lessons. On the top of my list is: If you don't really understand love, then don't tell people you love them. I found that I was only using that word to accomplish a sexual goal while the lady was using it to bond a relationship, for whatever motive she had. I think most of the time I said it I was not looking in their eyes, or if I was so dark that I could not see them anyway. So, in both our minds it was used as a means to an end. As I matured much later in life, I realized that not only was I using it for the wrong reasons, but "You only get out of it what you put into it!" So, for many years afterward, I went without using that four-letter word when expressing myself to women.

Another lesson: If you have any doubts about your love and your true commitment to the marriage, then do not marry. Like I said before, I got married because I thought it would be best for my children, especially my sons, and not because I was so deeply in love and wanted to spend my life with my wife. That was not right. I spent a lot of time trying to justify my feelings and trying to find a way out. I spent some time talking to my Godmother about loving my significant other. She told me that we all needed time to learn what love is and to get to know the person we think we are in love with.

She also told me that it takes time to really love someone. You may have to grow to love them, and most of the time, it is not easy. It takes commitment. I once heard someone call my Godmother a "Virtuous Woman." Well, I looked it up and found it to mean: *good, moral, honorable, worthy, and righteous.* Subconsciously, that is what I was looking for. I found it a few times in my life but did not realize it until it was too late!

Marriage also taught me about parenting. Parenting cannot be learned from a book; it is lived. I thought by getting married I would be raising my children in a stable home and safe environment. Not completely true.

Once I was told that my children could not come to the house when I was not home, a siren should have gone off in my head. But it was only a tiny little bell! After my Mom went home, Shari came to live with us. She was almost sixteen years old. I thought it was great, but I found out it was not. I had expected some female, mother-daughter types of attitudes and interactions, but this went beyond that. I thought that since my wife had been a single parent raising a daughter, she would understand. It was just the opposite. There was a lot of resentment, anger, jealousy, mistrust, and dislike between the two.

When the children got together it was a joyous time. You heard laughter, playing, and happiness; at least that was the way it was when I was there. I would sit down with the three of them and plan the weekly dinner menus and activities. By this time Myra, my eldest daughter, was grown and had her own apartment.

Well, one day my wife told me that I could not cook in her kitchen. After a lengthy discussion, I ignored that. We finally talked again on the subject and compromised. I told her to cook what she wanted us to eat that evening before she went to work. Sometimes she did, but it was not enough. So, me and the children went back to our round table talks.

I would make sure the meals were healthy with very little fast food. We would do homework together, discuss their problems and concerns and, when somebody got in trouble, decide the punishment to fit the crime. I learned a lot about parenting and building their confidence in me to protect them and take care of them. I already knew a lot from helping to raise my brothers and sisters but there was a lot more to it.

We built that certain bond and trust where they knew I was fair and impartial, compassionate and sympathetic, but stern and would protect them at all costs. My sons are introverts like me, so I tried to set forums for them to speak. I didn't have that problem with my girls. I actually had to remind them that they were ladies. They would say things that made their brothers and me blush. I once told them that they should talk like I was right behind them because they did not know who knew their parents and grandparents. Those girls had a mouth on them!

In all, they knew they could speak their minds because I encouraged that. The only rule was "they had to be respectful." That was totally unheard of when I was growing up. At that time, "children were seen and not heard."

Things were working out in some respects, but other things were going terribly wrong. One night I got home from working at Chuckie Cheese and my wife told me that she and Shari had some words. I was not really surprised or upset about that. What I got upset about was what she said next.

She said she was going to go in and beat her. Well, I was opposed to that! Don't get me wrong, I had no opposition to disciplining her, but not 12 hours after it happened. I told her that and all hell broke loose! The next morning, I talked to Shari about it. She gave me her side of the story and said she wanted to go live with her Mom. I disagreed with that decision, but I felt it was best for her safety.

Shari went to live with her Mom, but that did not work out the way she thought it would. She started missing classes and school and her grades dropped. I was constantly checking on her without her knowledge. When prom time came in the 12th grade, I told her that I would not buy her a prom dress and she could not go to the prom. I explained to her that the prom was a reward and she did not deserve to go.

She did not like that and started being very sassy and loud. I told her to stand in front of the van so we could just end it all right then. She ran into one of her friend's houses. The friend's mother told me I should let her go to the prom and I told her if she wanted her to go then she should pay for it. I also explained about her grades in school and that she was not going to graduate.

Well, she did not believe me, but Shari did not graduate. That summer she got herself together and went to an alternative school. She completed her high school requirements the next year. She was at the top of her class and asked for a reward. I replied to her that she would get no reward for doing what she should have done the year before.

A few years later, when Sylvester Jr. was almost sixteen years old, we started having little father/son issues. It started with him cutting class.

He went to Carver Vocational Technical High School. In his 10th grade year, he was starting his major in Carpentry. He came to me and asked if he could take carpentry. His explanation was, "You always talk about having to get a carpenter to do the work, so if I take carpentry, we'll have a carpenter." That was great to hear from him. Remember he is an introvert. He thought this out and came to me for approval. "YES!" I was happy with that decision, as he is a very talented person when he sets his mind to it.

So, at fifteen years old, he was already familiar with the basics of plumbing, HVAC, electricity, and now he was learning carpentry. Then it happened. I took him to school one morning and after stopping to see Mr. Murdock, who lived near there, I drove back past the school and he was out on the basketball court across the street from the school. It was mid-morning, not lunchtime.

I stopped the van and talked to the school police. I identified myself and informed him of what was about to take place. He said, "Roger that." I started walking toward my son on the court and thinking he was going to come toward me. He took off running in the opposite direction.

I took one or two steps to run after him and got a charley-horse in my leg, so I could not pursue him. Embarrassed, I limped back to the van and continued my pursuit. He was gone. I got home and told my wife about what had just happened. She denied that it was him out there as he was in his class.

Well, when he got home that afternoon, I sat him down and discussed the incident with him. I just told him that I understood he did not want to look bad in front of his mother, but he could at least apologize to me. He got really angry and looked like he wanted to hit me. I then went on to explain to him about life choices and consequences. I explained to him about crossing over into manhood and what could or would happen to him if he addressed or approached a man in a threatening manner. I told him the next time he ran from me I would not give up the chase, because men keep going until we accomplish our task.

A few weeks went by and my wife and I were sitting on the porch eating crabs while talking. She told me that my son had anger issues and that if I ever got in his face again, I would see what he would do to me. I told her that she and her Mom should never address nor encourage that type of conversation. Now, remember this: my son was a nationally ranked junior martial artist. I trained him in karate and my cousin, Jerome Featherstone, taught him wrestling. He excelled in both. So I knew how vicious he could get. He came home and was huffing and puffing, mad at the world!

I spoke and asked what was wrong. He blew up and told me: "I don't understand." I asked him to sit down so we could talk about it and he pulled away from me in anger. So I started the conversation with him again, telling him he had until the count of five, in which all my fingers would be closed. (That would tell me he wanted to fight and I would hit him. And it would not be over until I said it was over.)

While I was counting, I was praying, "God, please settle him down. Please don't let me have to continue this!" God answered my prayer that night and we were able to sit down and talk.

But a couple of weeks later, all hell broke loose. It was the Ravens' first game since moving to Baltimore and my friend,

Jerry Boorts, got tickets for the game. This was my first time ever attending a professional football game, even though I had played football for most of my life. My uncle Jason used to take me to the then Baltimore Colts' training camp, but I had never seen a real game at the stadium. Jason was a good friend of Lenny Moore, #24, halfback.

We were on the way to the game and I received a phone call from my wife. She was in a panic saying my son had gone off, thrown her against the refrigerator, and torn up the basement. So, we turned around and went back to the house. I found my son in the basement still very angry. We sat down and talked. I explained to him that his behavior, although I understood his frustration, was unacceptable. He kept referring to his Mother as "her" and "she" and I kept correcting him, as calm as I could, that his mother was not to be referred to in that manner.

So, when I thought I had gotten through and he was calm, I told him to clean up the mess he made in the basement and when I got back from the game, we would go out somewhere. He started to walk away from me, ignoring what I just said. So, I said to him: "Didn't we just have this conversation about your attitude and behavior?" He answered with a spinning back fist.

I fell back and slipped on the water and cologne that spilled in the tussle. I almost went down to the floor. I regained my balance and it was on between him and me.

My wife was screaming for Jerry to come. By the time Jerry got there, I had subdued him and put him to sleep. She was still screaming, "You're killing him." I said, "No, this is my son. I am just putting him to sleep."

I let him go and went to walk away, but he came after me again. I caught him with a spinning back kick and then I went after him. When he realized that I was getting the best of him, he looked around and ran out the backdoor. When he looked around, I was right behind him.

We went up into the alley, between the houses, and down the front of the houses. He ran to his friend's house, up the long flight of stairs, through the house, and out the back door. I was still behind him. He ran back toward the house and his Mom had Myra waiting in her car to take him to her mother's house. That was where he continued to stay.

I explained to her mother what happened and told her that I would not allow him to disrespect me, his mother, or any other adult in my house or anywhere else. I told her if she wanted to raise him by her rules then he needed to stay in her house. That week she had my wife arrested for child abuse. My wife was upset because she chose to accept a plea bargain, even though I provided an attorney, and received one year of supervised probation, a fine, and parenting classes, as I had told her would happen. Each time she went to see our son she came back crying because they treated her so badly. I never went down there or sent any money.

She had me arrested for the same charge a few months later. The Maryland State Troopers' Fugitive Task Force, the military police, my special operation and response team, and federal agents came to my job to arrest me. General Counsel contacted me and advised me of my rights, that I did not have to go with them because I was on federal government property. I agreed to go with them and General Counsel went with me to make sure my rights were not abused.

I was transported to Baltimore City Detention Center, not far from my house, and placed in a cell overnight. The Trooper that transported me understood what had taken place and decided to stay with me until it was time for his shift to end. I was released on my own merit. Both my wife and mother-in-law were upset about that.

It took me three years to fight them in court and have the case finally dismissed. By this time my son had turned eighteen years old and when he was asked if he still wanted to pursue it, he said no. That did not sit well with his mother and grandmother. My nightmare was over, but the great thing that came out of it was I finally got the opportunity to talk about what happen and to share with him the lessons that could be learned from it.

My son dropped out of high school and never managed to go back and complete it. Many times I offered him the opportunity to get into the Plumbing Trade School as an apprentice. But each time I mentioned that he would have to get a high school equivalence certificate to be eligible, he refused. Some years later, Shari told me that maybe I was trying to force my will on him. I listened to her and apologized to Sylvester Jr. I explained to him that I was trying to help him by using the only connections and skills that I had to offer at that time. And that is all I will say about that.

As I said before, my sons were in karate and wrestling. Kenneth did not like physical sports like those, but I required it for three years. His Mom put him in Little League baseball. I was not that much up on baseball, even though my Mom loved it but I could play. I supported all that came with it.

I knew some of the coaches from the Lodge. There he met his best friend and my adopted son, Jerae. After baseball, my wife put him in football. I felt more at home there, because I had played for a lot of years before moving to karate and kickboxing. Football is where Kenneth found his talent. When he was on the sidelines, you did not know he was there. But once he took the field, everybody knew he was there. He played linebacker and ran fullback, and he was very strong.

He played football and lacrosse after he got to Northwestern High School. He was one of the captains on the team in his second year. I got to know his coaches and worked with some of the players in the summer, at Kenneth's request, before the season started. The only incident I had with Kenneth was when he got the car.

It started when I was in Qatar. I received an email from his Mom asking me to call her. I was in the middle of the desert and phones were not readily accessible. When I got thru to her, she asked if I would help buy Kenneth a car. I disagreed with that idea. I told her that he was becoming a good athlete and a car would become a distraction and get him in trouble. He got the car and, after a little while, he had his first accident.

When I came home from a temporary tour of duty (TDY), I went to a practice and I didn't see him. I talked to the Coach and he told me my son had regularly missed practices. I waited for him to come home one night and met him. I started to ask him about how football was going. He started telling me how things were going well and before I knew it, I had thrown him against the car.

I told him to never lie to me and that I had been out to his team practice and talked to the Coach. I reminded him that he was supposed to set the example as the team captain and be out there, even if he was injured. If I were the Coach, I would fire him and bench him! Well, he got the message; at least for a while.

Then in his senior year, he made the All Maryland State Athlete Football Team. I had been working a lot and traveling, so I did not make all of the practices. I went out there at the next to last practice and I did not see Kenneth. I talked to the Coach and he said he had gotten injured and had taken a couple of days off.

Well, I did not go to the extent as before, but I told him he was jeopardizing his chances to let the college coaches see him perform. On game day, they are only required to let the players play a quarter, and that is what happened. He only played a quarter and they sat him down for the rest of the game. His Mom was screaming and yelling for them to put him in, but she did not know what was happening, even now!

Myra was a lot less dramatic than her siblings; she is ten years older than Shari. I missed the first seven to eight years of her life. I started working with her in karate and she was really good. Even though she was very skinny, she was very strong. Our relationship grew from there.

Myra went to Carver Vocational Technical High School and had plans to become an architect. Low and behold in her junior year, she decided she wanted to be a cosmetologist. I tried to persuade her to go the other way and just do hair on the side. I even put in a shampoo bowl for her. But it did not happen. Then she got pregnant in the 12th grade, but she did graduate with her class. For some reason, I was not invited to the graduation.

Martiez, my first grand-child, was born the September after her graduation. That was a proud and painful moment for me. When I was looking at her future, I did not see a grandchild that early. I was determined not to accept the idea of Myra having a child. I did not want to help her take care of him or hold him. I just did not want to acknowledge how much I loved my grandson.

One day, in the early afternoon, I was lying across the bed when she asked me to watch Martiez while she went to do something. I did not say yes or no. I was just being a jerk, so she put him on the bed beside me. He was crawling at that time and I really wanted to play with him but just wouldn't. I remember mumbling to him, like he understood what I was saying, "You better lay down. You better stop jumping." Then he fell off the bed and hit the floor.

Before he even cried out, Myra was back upstairs. She grabbed him from me and took him with her. She gave me a look that I had never seen before and never wanted to see again. After that, she never asked me to watch him, put him on the bed beside me, or left him in the room with me again. I really felt bad about how I felt I was acting. I finally outgrew my childish act. Martiez was a great child and grew up to be a great man.

I always tried to stay firm in my parenting decisions. For what it is worth, I always tried and try to be the parent who is loving, caring, compassionate, fair, respectful, stern, and no-nonsense but fun. The parent who demands that his children be respectful and courteous to adults, to each other, and to others. The standards I have set and demonstrated are the same ones that I pray my children live by and demand from others.

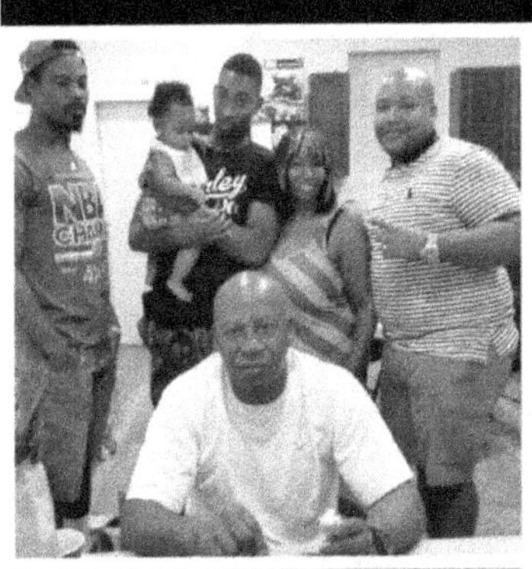
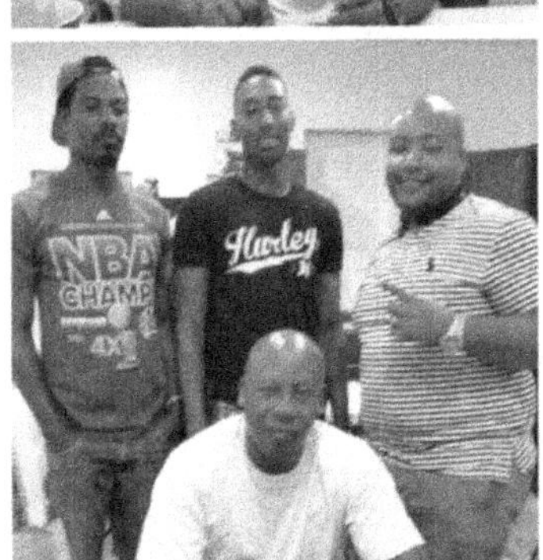

Jazmine's Wedding 2019

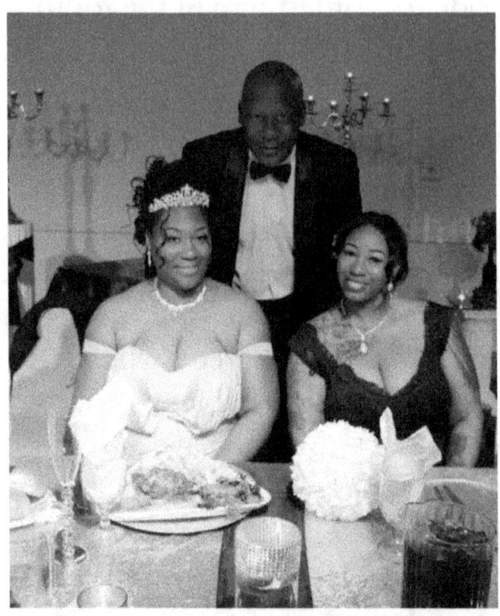

Jaz, Shari, & Ken

Malik, Shari, & Martiez 2019

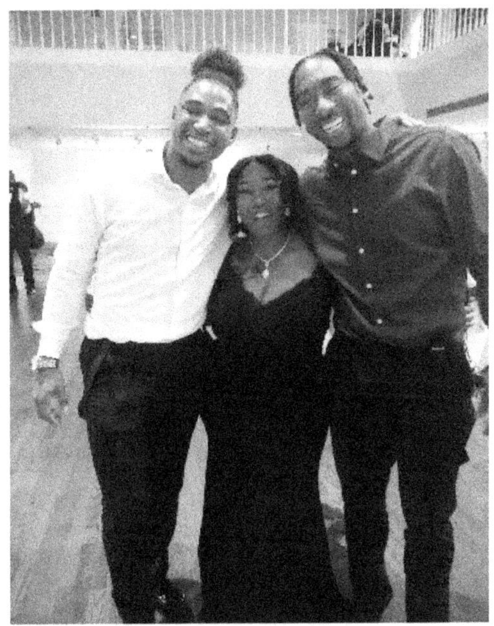

Keon 2019   **Tamyra 2020**

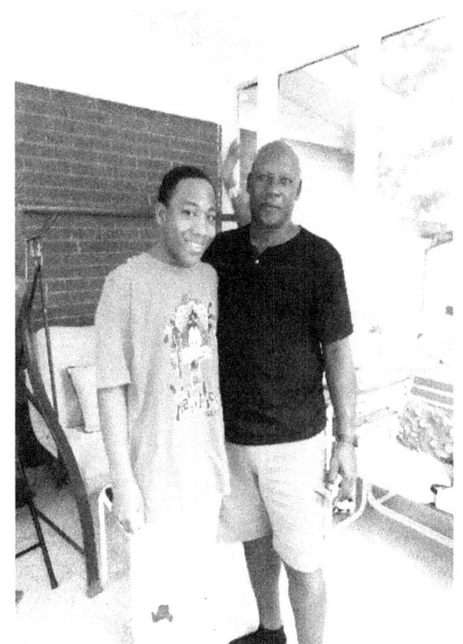

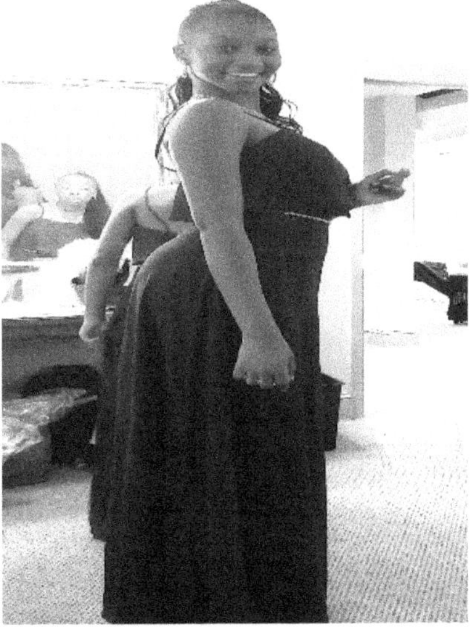

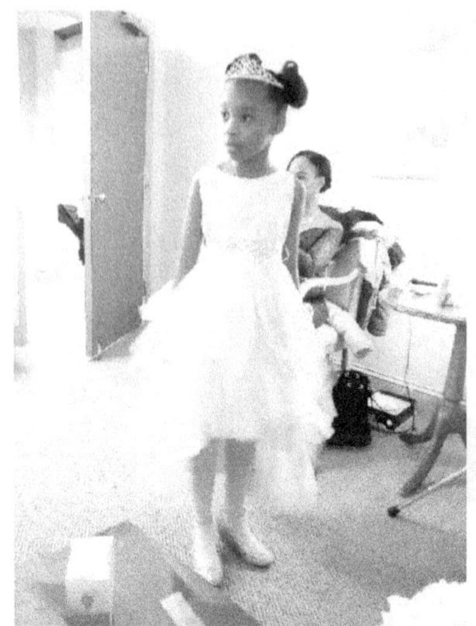

Haden 2020

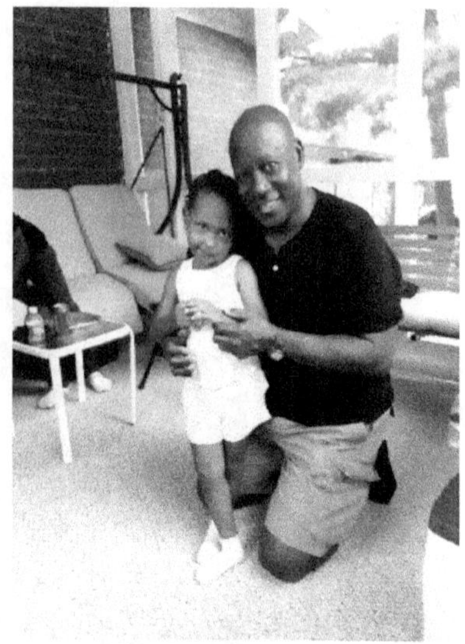

Max 2019

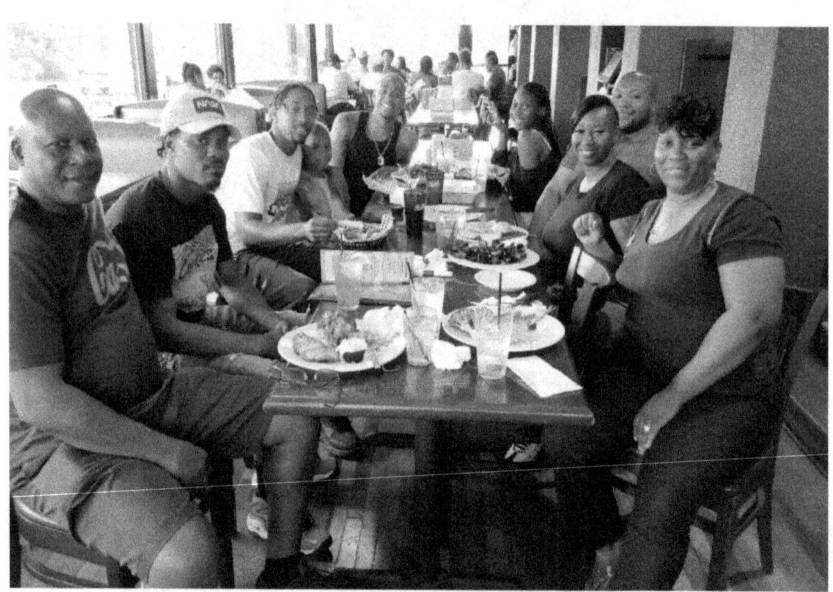

Baltimore 2018

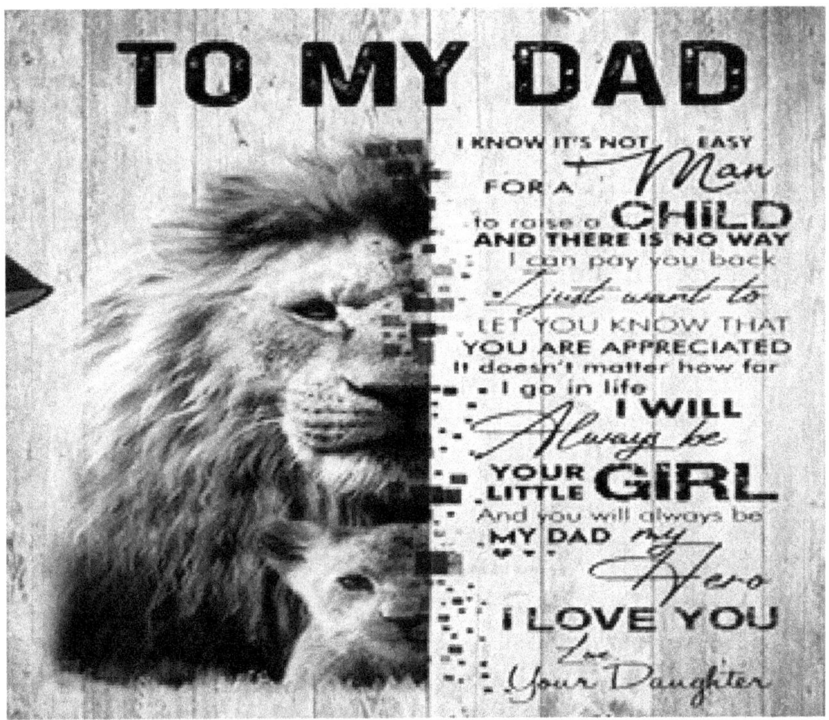

Cash, Keith Pam, Debbie, Anthony (Dennis MIA)

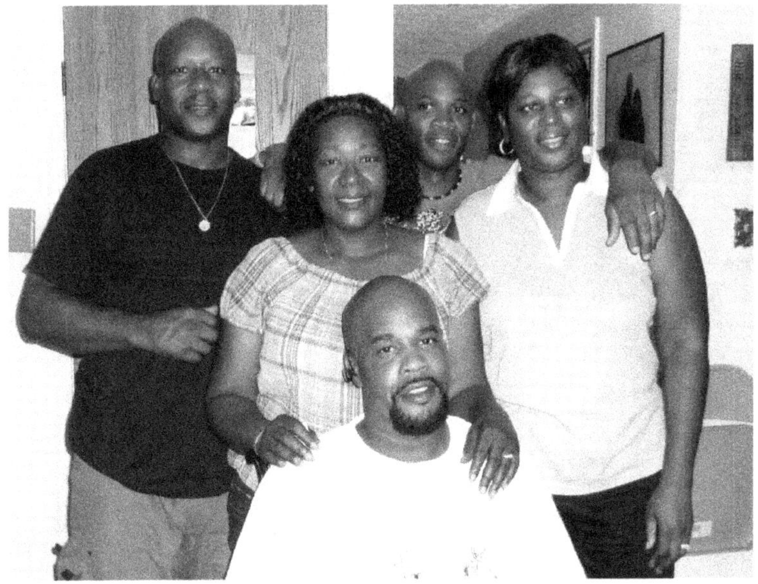

Older sisters Celestine, Lorthea Mae, and Cora Mae

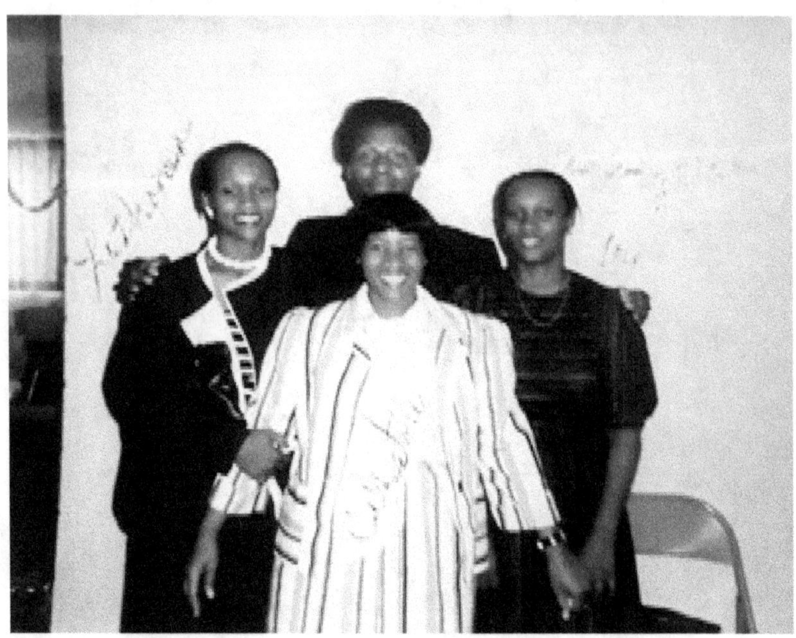

Dad and some of his children: Celestine, Angel, Cora Mae, Me, grandchildren

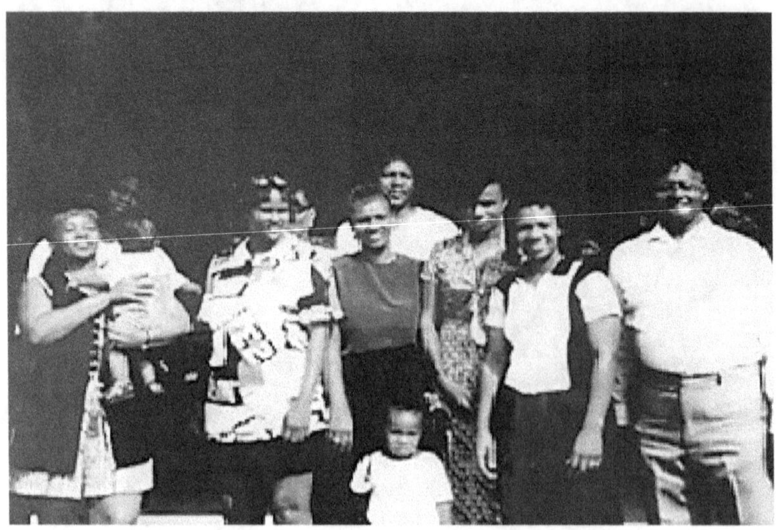

Pope Family 2018

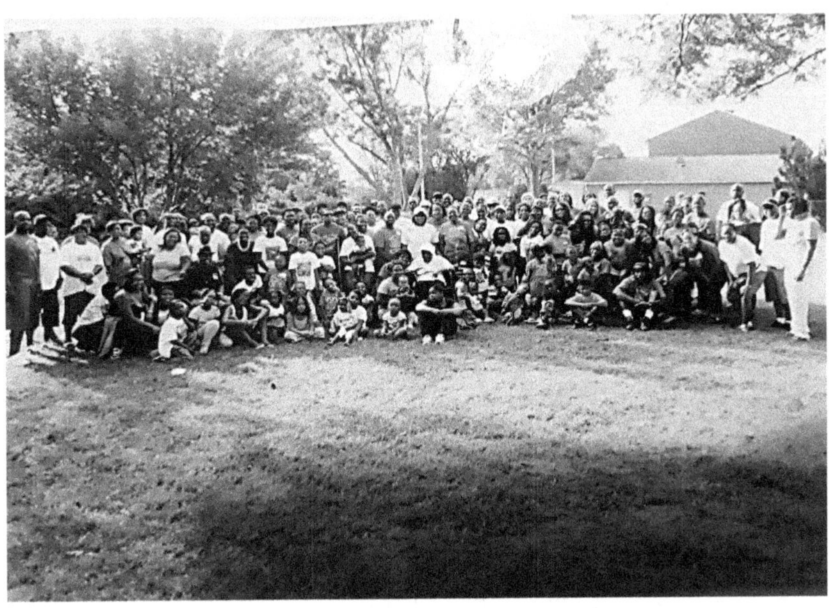

"IN THE BEGINNING"

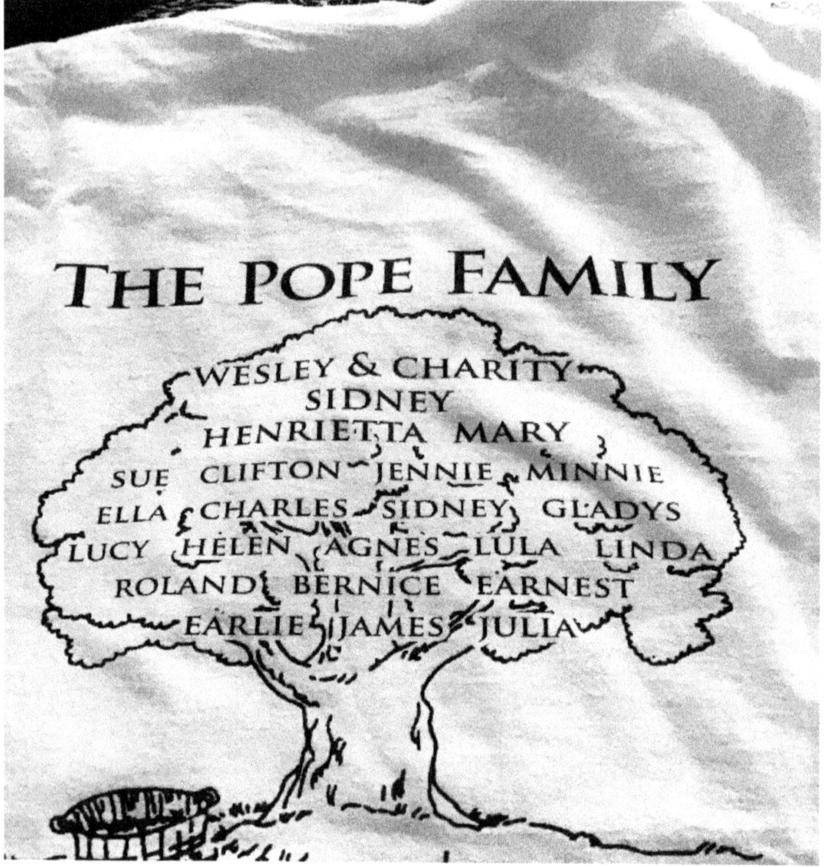

OUR LINEAGE

AGNES POPE (MOTHER)

Sylvester Cash

Pamela Lloyd (Banchett)

Debbie Mashelle Powell

Anthony Pope

Bryan Keith Pope

Dennis Pope

Stephen Alexander Wilson (Deceased)

ABRAHAM CASH (FATHER)

Brothers and Sisters

Willie Cash

Celestine Cash Brumley

Lotharen Cash Craig

Cora Mae Cash Conley

Loretta Cash

Maxine Sanders

Angela Sandes

Angela Cash

Charlene Cash (Deceased)

Willie Kinard

<u>SYLVESTER CASH SR.</u>

<u>Children, grandchildren, and great-grandchildren</u>

Myra Ann Cypress a.k.a Jazman Cash-03/12/xxxx

Martiez Reed-09/7/1989

Haden Reed-07/15/2011

Arianna Reed-03/28/2019

Darnell Davis-1/12/1994

Kyrie Davis-06/10/2016

Daniyah Davis-11/5/2017

Malik Davis-07/13/1995

Shari Andrea Jennings-08/03/xxxx

Sylvester Cash Jr.-11/02/xxxx

Tamyra Steward-10/16/2005

Kenneth Cash-10/18/xxxx

Keon Cash-02/3/2004

Maxwell Olivia Cash-11/7/2014

Chapter 3

Military

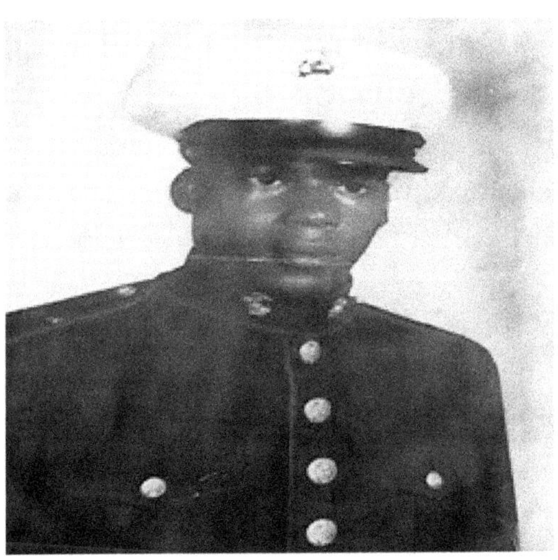

My military career began in March 1973 when I enlisted in the Marine Corps under the 180-day delay program. I never talked to my Momma about doing this; I just did it. Like I said before, I never talked to her about the things going on in my life or decisions I was about to make. I was introduced to the Marine Corps by Mr. Charles, who was a former Force Recon Marine. The time, training, and discipline inspired me to want to be like him, a Marine.

Although I was in my senior year of high school and my Momma was very supportive, I still never felt confident enough to talk to her. She attended all the home football games, got my tuxedo for my Senior Prom. She even let my friend Penn use her car to take me to the Prom. Deep down inside I knew that she really cared about me and my happiness, but I could not acknowledge it openly. I think when I finally told her I had enlisted in the Marine Corps, she was probably relieved on one hand and angry and disappointed on the other because I had not confided in her. I know that it is too late to say it, but I truly apologize, Momma!

There are times still in my life that I wish I would have talked to her about things going on with me. I wish I would have just told her how much I loved her and appreciated everything that she did for me. You never realize how great your Momma is until she is gone and you think back over your life and reality sets.

There was talk going around that I might get a football scholarship from North Carolina A&T. We already knew that Ricky Moore, our quarterback, was definitely going and he did. Me? I was not as certain and I really did not want to go back to school anyway. So, I enlisted in the Marine Corps. I had turned nineteen years old, so I did not need my Momma to sign for me. When I finally told Momma, I really never knew how she took it, because as I stated earlier, we didn't talk much about my future plans. But I was excited!

The weekend before I left, Momma gave me a going-away party. I don't remember us talking about it, but she made it happen. All of my local relatives and neighborhood friends were there. To my surprise, the party lasted all weekend, at least for me and some of my friends. Momma never said a thing! Even on the morning that I left for boot camp, she never said a word. She did not even come down to see me off! I guess this was her way of allowing me to be my own man and not babying me!

So, bright and early Wednesday morning on August 22, 1973, I left my house on Holmes Avenue and walked to the United States Marine Corps Recruiting Station at Mondawmin Mall. There I reunited with my school friend and football buddy, Cleveland. I was surprised to see him. He never told us that he had enlisted. From that point, we tried to support and encourage one another all through boot camp.

The recruiter met us there and we boarded a bus that took us to the Armed Forces Examination Entry Station (AFEES) at BWI Airport, the military processing station. At the processing station, we were given packages and put on a plane to South Carolina. I was still recovering from the party, so I do not remember what all took place there! After, getting off the plane we got onto a bus that took us to an island in South Carolina. I truly had no idea where I was at or where we were headed. Later that night, we finally arrived at the Parris Island Recruit Depot in Beaufort County, South Carolina, to begin my basic training.

The Drill Instructor came on the bus and welcomed us "to the land that God forgot!" In a loud, friendly, and commanding voice, he told us in no Christian words, to get our bodies off the bus and get on the footprints! We were met by two more Drill Instructors, screaming in our ears and all up in our faces.

We were then marched into a waiting room. We were told that there was only one way on and one way off the island. I remember silence coming over that room from that point on. It was just a time of extreme chaos. I just kept thinking that at the end of Basic Training, I would be a Marine and be sent to fight in the Vietnam War. But it didn't matter—I needed to help Momma and my family.

That night, we were given a box lunch and then given some linen and a blanket. My first night. I knew that we were all tired and worn out from the plane and bus rides, but most of us did not sleep very soundly. I was scared just like everybody else of what might come up next.

That morning we were awakened by loud barreling voices. We were told what to do, how to do it, and when to do it. After breakfast, we were marched to the barbershop. The haircuts that we got were fast and clean down to the scalp. There were no fads, no, a little off here or there, just straight and to the point BALD! Then we were taken to supply and issued shower supplies, towels, shower shoes, shaving gear, clothes, boots, and tennis shoes. We filled out more paperwork and got more physical examinations. Things went so fast that day I never remembered having lunch or dinner.

Through the next few days, we formally met our Drill Instructors. We were told to each write a letter to our families. In the letters, we were told what to tell them and that was it. The Drill Instructors looked them over to make sure they were what they said and that no one added anything else. From that point on we belonged to them. As I said earlier, we were told what to do, when to do it, and how to do it. Everything was by the numbers. There were no favorites and everybody was treated the same and spoken to the same, at least in the beginning. We were all the lowest form of life and all GREEN!

As time went on that changed a little—we became maggots, scums of the earth, and other descriptive forms of low life. After a couple of days, the weak were weeded out from the strong and the leaders rose to the top of the barrel. The Drill Instructors were always tough and always "squared away." They used language that I had never heard before in my life. Some of the things they would say to you would be really funny, but you better not laugh. Some of the things they would say to you or about you would make you either want to lash out at them or make you want to cry, but you better not show any emotions or attempt to do anything in retaliation.

In boot camp, we were always competing and the competition was heavy. I was at the head of my platoon from the start. I was a squad leader and then the platoon guide. They would juggle you around in the platoon to mess with your mind and try to humiliate you. I was able to withstand these actions and compete with the best in my platoon, who were from all over the United States and all walks of life. Once the hierarchy was established, we had each other's backs. When one got punished, we all got punished! We motivated each other and carried one another's weight when it was needed.

The Drill Instructors would do all kinds of things to shake you up or break your spirit. After a while, I understood that! I remember saying to myself, "This is all they got? My Momma was worse than this!" I came to fear only one thing on Parris Island and that was "Seven Day Motivation." If you were unmotivated and a constant screwed-up, they would send you first to One Day Motivation. If you continued then it would be Three Day Motivation and the final step was Seven Day Motivation. After that, there was no hope of you conforming or adjusting to Marine Corps life, so you were "DROPPED/ Send Home".

They would bring the Motivation Squad into the chow hall and they looked and smelled like pigs. They wanted to put the fear of God in us to see firsthand, what life would be like if we did not conform or kept screwing up. It did it for me! If they did not get enough people to send there, they would unknowingly to you have you volunteer. It almost happened to me one day.

The Drill Instructor came in looking for volunteers and me, being motivated and ready to do anything over and beyond, raised my hand. He picked right over me and I remember getting upset because I knew I was better than the ones he chose. Then he said, "Congratulations. You maggots have just volunteered for One Day Motivation. Get your gear!" This indescribable feeling came over me and I was cautious from that point on what I volunteered for.

I heard that they were made to crawl through sewage ditches and they shot live rounds over their head to make them keep their faces in the sewage. They ran everywhere they went and when they came to the Chow Hall, they had to eat their food by the numbers and a whistle. The instructors were merciless and the recruits were not treated like humans. I thought to myself that if I ever got sent there, I would take my chances trying to get off of the island.

Even though they had already told us and showed us pictures of recruits that had tried to escape and had been killed and eaten by the alligators, crabs, and fish in the swamp, I was still going to try to get off. Later I found out that what would get you killed would be high tide. The island was bigger than we thought and, in the evening, the high tide would rush in unexpectedly and you would get caught in the undercurrent and drown or the alligators would get you. But if you were lucky enough to make it off of the island, the upstanding local citizens of Beaufort, South Carolina would turn you into the authorities and collect a reward from the Corps.

During my training, I received a few minor injuries and strains but nothing serious enough to stop me from completing the training. Exercising is a major part of boot camp. Our days would start with physical training (PT). The whole program including the entire day was mapped out. When things got slow or ahead of schedule, we would just do more PT. The exercises that we did were not anything new or hard if you worked out. They were the same exercises that you did if you played football, ran track or cross country, played baseball, wrestled, or swam. They were just called different names. Some of the names would amuse you and some would intimidate you.

One thing about boot camp was the language used. It was not the kind of language you would use around your Momma, minister, or children. We would do pushups, sit-ups, leg lifts, bends, and thrusts, but that was not what they were called. They called these exercises mountain climbers, side-straddle hops, or jumping jacks. The ones that I think I really hated the most were the bends and thrusts or (bends and mother f**kers) and the mountain climbers.

When you were doing PT as a disciplinary or motivational activity, there was no pleasure only pain and sweat. The Drill

Instructors would say things like, "I am going to PT you until I get tired." You ask yourself, *How is he going to get tired he is not doing anything but watching?* You would tell yourself to keep going until you filled the circle with sweat and the circle would cover the entire squad bay.

Then at night after you showered and thought you had escaped something you messed up on that day, they would call you to the Quarter Deck and the fun would begin. We had one thing they called watching TV. That was one of the worst things I ever encountered. It was worse than the leg lifts, bends, and mother f**kers combined.

They would ask who wanted to watch TV. Not seeing a TV in weeks and being stupid, we would raise our hands. The instructor would call us up to the Quarter Deck and have us get down in the prone position, only supporting ourselves by our toes and elbows under our chin. We were on a concrete floor, profusely sweating and he would be cracking jokes, asking us questions, or telling us to change the channel. Mind you, to change the channel, you would have to lift one of your elbows off the floor and reach out as to change the channel or make any adjustments.

You would find yourself balancing on one elbow with your hand under your chin, one on your leg while you were sweating and the floor was getting slippier and slippier. The instructor would start telling you to find imaginable football games, ask you the score, and then tell you to find a game with the score he tells you or that his team is winning. After a few months into training, it became fun for some and challenging for others. Every time that you fall, the time starts over. After boot camp, I would not watch TV for a very long time, I just went to the movies.

Then, after a run one morning, I came down with pneumonia. I was admitted to the hospital for over a week. My Drill Instructor came to see me and told me that if I was not back to the platoon within seven days, I would be recycled. I tried every way I could to get back to my platoon. I constantly thought about my friend from high school, Cleveland, who came in with me. I felt that I needed to be there for him and the platoon; we were family! Well, I did not get out of the hospital in time and, as a result, I was recycled to another platoon after being discharged. This meant an additional two weeks or more of training to graduate.

When I got to the new platoon, I had to re-establish myself. That was not very hard for me to do and I think that my last Drill Instructor had told them about me, which might have helped. But this still did not make things easy for me. The Drill Instructors already had established a relationship with the squad leaders, so every chance they got they threw me to the back of the platoon and I had to work my way back to the front.

When we got to our 3rd and final phase of training, we moved to the rifle range for two weeks. I remember watching my original platoon leaving the range to prepare for graduation. But I had other things to worry about while at the Rifle Range. I was competing for the number one slot again. I had never fired a rifle before so this was challenging. We knew that the one with the highest score out of the squad leaders and platoon guide would get dress blues and private first class. I wanted those dress blues and wanted them bad!

It seemed like one of the Drill Instructors was all over me, all the time. One night he had me up on the Quarter Deck and punched me in the solar plexus. I did not go down. Then he asked me if I wanted to strike him back. And, not being stupid, I said "SIR, NO SIR!" That night, after lights went out, the squad leaders came to me and asked if I wanted them to take care of him. I said no. But it made me feel good that they had embraced me as a brother.

This was the first time I had ever fired a real rifle. I was quite nervous and shaky. I tried not to let it show. As the week progressed, I was shooting well and shooting in the expert range. I just knew I would ace this course. I was feeling that the dress blues were in my grasp.

Thursday was prequalification day and I shot expertly. I was overjoyed; it was in the bag. Friday came and I was on the last unit to shoot. I started out shooting fairly well on the 200-yard line and then everything went south. I was on the 300-yard line and was not hitting anything—miss after miss after miss! I repeatedly checked my body alignment, my sight picture, and my breathing. Nothing was helping.

When I got back to the 500-yard line, I immediately realized that. I was not going to qualify. I was so upset, I just wanted to crawl into a ball and cry.

 "Why me?" I kept asking myself. I got down in the prone position and settled in and hit nothing but bull's eyes. At that point, it was still not enough. Not only did I not get the dress blues, but I did not make PFC out of boot camp. To this day I do not know what happened! I Almost Made It! It was a long lonely march back to the barracks.

When we returned from the rifle range, I watched my original platoon graduate from my barracks. I remember the tears rolling from my eyes because I was not out there with them! Afterward, I was informed that they would be the last platoon to be sent to Vietnam. I remember feeling I had missed out on one of the very reasons that I became a Marine, and now I would not be able to make the extra money that I'd hoped to help my family. **I Almost Made It!**

After boot camp, I was assigned to the 2nd Shore Party Battalion, 2nd Marine Division at Camp Lejeune, North Carolina. At Shore Party, we were recognized by the red patches on our trousers and cover.

The red patch dates back to the early days of WWII during the Battle of Guadalcanal. After the initial assault on the beachhead, the troops came ashore and the confusion on the beach led to the creation of a Landing Support Marine unit. This unit became known as Shore Party. However, some Shore Party Marines went inland along with the Infantry (Grunt) Battalions to set-up Landing Zones for supplies and medical evacuations.

When we 'grunts' hit the beach, we would get attached to special units and hump with them. They were constantly on the move and you had to be in shape to keep up with them.

I remember, one night, waking up and they were gone. I almost panicked, then I remembered I was a Field Radio

Operator and I had a radio. All I had to do was call my unit and they would send somebody to come get me. Well, the only problem I had was I had no idea where I was at!

Lucky for me, the First Sergeant came back and got me. Well, that never happened to me again. I slept with one eye open and both ears to the ground. Anything that moved, I was moving too. It was quite an adventure for me, though I never told anyone.

I gained great respect for the grunts after being attached to them on several occasions. They were a tight-knit group and cared for each other. They were a wild and crazy bunch at times, but you had to be mentally and physically strong to do the job they were asked to do.

As I said earlier, the 2nd Shore Party Battalion was responsible for supporting Marine ground forces by setting up Landing Zones for helicopters to bring in troops, supplies, ammunition, and equipment and evacuate the wounded. We were also responsible for setting up very large command post tents, putting up large poles, and digging trenches for running miles and miles of communication wire through the air and underground. This was for our local communication networks onshore and maintaining communications with Command ships, helicopters, and ground forces 24 hours a day.

Manning the radios, Lt. Ketchall, Cash, Tony Hall, Mike Pope 1976

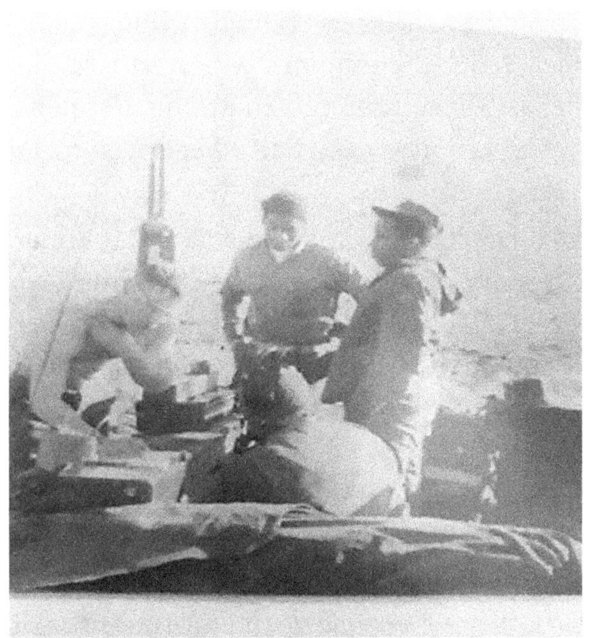

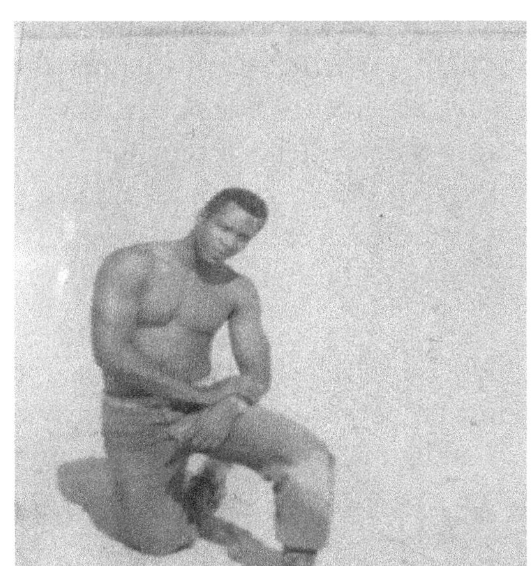

You were up long hours manning the radios and maintaining other communication equipment so that communications were maintained with all the essential elements for the units on the beach at all times. Being in this special unit, we had to rappel from helicopters when no landing zone was available, so I was required to attend Rappelling Schools at Ft. Steward, Georgia, and San Diego, California.

We also did desert training and survival training for six weeks each year in the Mojave Desert at 29 Palms, California. While in the desert, we would often hike 10-20 miles a week. That was pretty rough walking fully loaded through the shifting sand.

I was sent to Field Radio Operator School at Montford Point, another section located on Camp LeJeune. I remember thinking, "Oh no, not school again." I had not gone to college because I did not want to go to school anymore but look at me now: back to school. It was not as bad as I thought and I did quite well. My competition came from the guys in Recon Battalion—we called them Baby Recon because they were not Force Recon and they thought they were the best. Well, I became a Field Radio Operator and I was promoted to PFC finally. I also beat out those Baby Recon guys and it felt good!

Being a Field Radio Operator, you had to be in shape because you were required to carry not only your 60 lb. pack, 45 caliber handgun, M-16 rifle, and ammunition, but also your radio encryption unit and a three-day supply of extra batteries for each device.

The *KY-38* plus AN/PRC-77 radio with the battery alone weighed over 50 lbs. A three-day supply of batteries was an additional 9-plus lbs, plus three days of food and water. So, you could easily end up carrying over 100 lbs. on your back. I weighed around 175-180 lbs at that time and sometimes decided to do without extra clothing and food to lighten the load.

To stay in shape, I would run three to seven miles every other day and do hundreds of pounds of weight lifting in the gym with my new found friend and possible relative, Michael Pope. Mike was also a Radio Operator. He was from Raleigh, North Carolina and I know we had to be kin because my family is from Spring Hope, North Carolina and the last name was also Pope.

Mike was about 5 feet 7 inches tall and weighed about 140-145 lbs. He was fast, strong, smart, and very charismatic. Mike was running three miles in fifteen minutes, and that would be after he was out drinking and partying the night before.

When we went to the gym, he could leg press the entire amount on the weight machine. He never wanted to get his haircut. He always wanted to look good so he would pack his hair down with a stocking. He always looked sharp at inspections and in formation, but they would always get him for his hair.

Mike would max out the Physical Fitness Training (PFT) with 300 points. I was not as fast on the run as he was. I was only running three miles in 19:30 – 21 minutes. You needed to run 18:00 minutes or less to get 100 points, do 20 pull-ups, and then do 80 sit-ups in two minutes to score 300 points. So, I would end up with around 280-290 points each time. I didn't max the PFT until I was around 26 years old while in the Marine Corps Reserves. That was one of those 'I Made It!' moments.

Cash on USS Coronado 1974

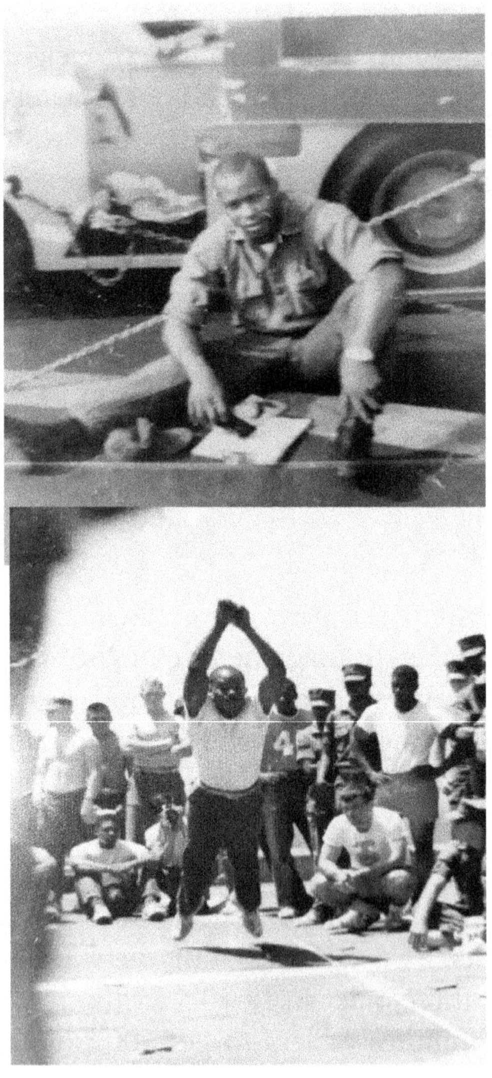

For some reason, I never wanted to get stationed overseas. Every time I heard that they were looking for someone to go to Okinawa, I would go out to the Mediterranean Sea, which we called the Med Cruise. My first trip as a young PFC was in 1974. I was deported to the 34th Marine Amphibious Unit on the USS Coronado LPD-11.

Before entering the Mediterranean Sea, we stopped in Roto, Spain. I had just turned twenty years old and it was my first time out of the United States. Wow, I could not believe I was in Spain, the first country that I ever visited. I had never even read about it in a book. Who would have ever thought I would be here? Not me. Not even in my wildest dreams!

Being from the ghetto of Baltimore City, I really did not know how to act or what I was expected to do. So, I just hung out with Mike and some of the other guys. It was "the blind leading the blind" but we never gave it a second thought.

All we were interested in were women and drinking! We were only there a few days so we did not get a chance to get into too much trouble. Things were always good for us because we were on the Flagship, and got into port or in better ports before the grunts. When the grunts landed, "there went the neighborhood" and the price of everything went up!

After we left Spain, we visited ports in Turkey, Greece, Italy, and North Africa, in operations with the local military forces. We worked on the beaches along with the Navy "Beach Masters", our Navy counterparts with Yellow Patches and Force Recon.

We were the only primitive unit on the beach, sleeping in tents and eating C- Rats! We would go to the water and catch small crabs, pick snails off the rocks, and boil them in our steel helmets with beer. That was fine dining! That steel pot came in handy. I would make stew by mixing the beef chunks or whatever meat you drew from the C-rats, pick onions from the surrounding vegetation, mix in some hot sauce, which only a few of us carried in our packs, and we had a meal. The Beach Masters and Recon had tents with cots, refrigerators, generators, and real silverware. They ate real food and desserts, and would sometimes share steaks and other food with us!

We got along great. I loved being on the same ship and beach with them! I particularly liked being around the Recon and Underwater Demolition Teams (UDT). I got to do a little training with them and see some of their toys. I learned a lot of things from them and found that most of them were highly educated, but down to earth. They were different from those Baby Recon guys I met in Comm School.

During the middle of our deportment, civil war broke out in Cyprus between the Greek and Turkish parts of the island. We sat off the coast for fifty days or more waiting to go ashore to assist. For weeks we lived out of our seabags on alert. Being a young PFC, I had no idea what was happening.

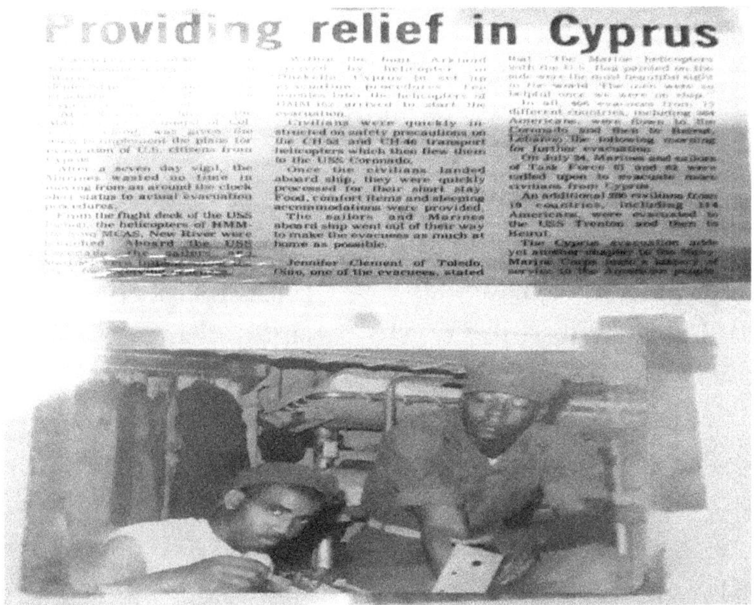

Evacuation of Cyprus 1974

Our Platoon Sergeant only gave us what we needed to know at that moment, and from my recollection, that was nothing! Then, one night, a couple of us were awakened and told to grab our gear—we were going in! My whole unit did not go, just the Radio Operators, a couple of Helicopter Support Team guys, and Special Forces personnel.

To this day, I do not know where we were at. We found dead bodies covered up, injured military personnel, and civilians. There was live gunfire still taking place outside of the compound. Within days, which felt like a week, we were able to secure the compound and evacuate Americans and civilians to our ships and then to Lebanon. I remember the joy in the sounds of their voices and smiles on the faces of the people we evacuated.

It was something that I had never seen before, just read about, or saw in the movies. I was only twenty years old and I have never forgotten the blood and smell of death that I experienced during that week.

I also remember not being able to sleep soundly, always fearing that someone would attack me in my sleep. For many years, I slept with some type of weapon near me, under my pillow, under the mattress, and in the chest of drawers. I still sleep lightly and awake when I hear the slightest noise, unless I have been drinking. Alcohol became my sedative when I wanted to sleep.

In 1976, it was time for rotations to Okinawa, and I was determined not to go there for thirteen months. So, in a move not to be selected, I volunteered to be deported to the 34th Marine Amphibious Unit in the Mediterranean Sea again. Once again, I got a chance to spend a little time in Spain, Italy, Turkey, and Greece. Then it happened again, conflict broke out. This time we were sent to Lebanon.

We joked to each other that "these are the same people we brought here from Cyprus, and we are taking them back home." We sat off the coast for 100 days before receiving orders to evacuate the Americans.

This was a one-day operation. We landed, organized, and prioritized the evacuees for helicopter extractions. We also provided medical attention to the injured and assisted in the preparation and removal of the dead.

I was almost 22 years old by this time. I had received three Meritorious Promotions. I was a Sergeant, E-5, and leader of the Communications section. I still remember not only the joy of those we evacuated but the faces of those that were killed as well as the crying of those injured. I remember having to try and prepare my men and talk to them about what we might encounter and what to expect of the evacuees. Those are two deployments I will never forget!

After that deportment, I knew that I was too short (didn't have enough time left) to be selected for a tour in Okinawa, so life became more normal. I got back in time to play football. Once again, for the fourth straight year, I made the All-Marine Team. I played football, softball, and ran track, along with weightlifting and cross-country during my entire time in the Marine Corps, football was my favorite. I played running back and linebacker. I was offered a tryout for a Semi-Pro team in Baltimore once I left active duty.

All Marine Football Team 1974-77

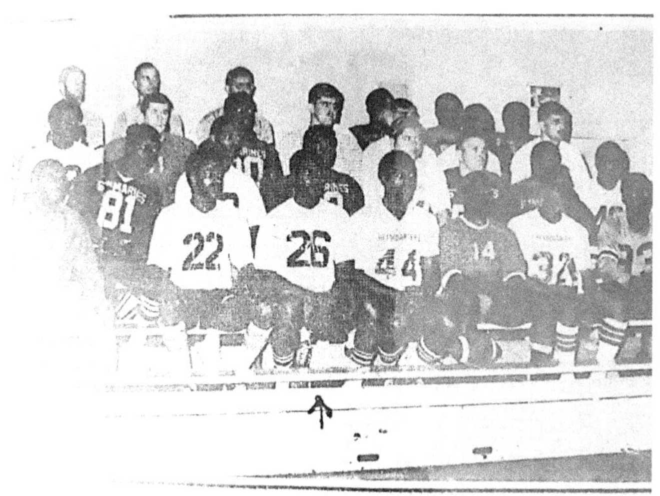

With that offer on the table, I looked forward to the day when I was reported. Even though the Recon Football team broke my ankle in the championship game, I was still able to rehabilitate in time for the season.

In my last year on active duty as an expert marksman, I worked on the Rifle Range as the Battalion Range Coach, also as the NCOIC of Range Coaches for the 2nd Shore Party Battalion. The Commanding Officer had promised me that as long as everyone qualified on the Rifle Range, life would be easy for me. So, I made sure that happened. I enjoyed that job and spent most of my time at the range. The only time I was not at the Range was when I was competing in some sporting event for the unit.

When the time came for me to be released from active duty, I did not want to go, but I wanted to pursue my football career. I avoided all ceremonies. They really did not know I had left until I came back the next year with the Reserves. I had gotten good at not being seen.

After getting settled in Shore Party, promotions came quickly for me. After I graduated from boot camp in November of 1973, I was promoted to Private First Class; E-2 in March of 1974 then promoted to Lance Corporal; E-3, then Meritorious Corporal; E-4 in January 1975; Meritorious Sergeant, E-5 in March 1976. After leaving active duty and joining the Marine Corps Reserves, in May 1980, I was promoted to Staff Sergeant, E-6; all in a total of fewer than seven years…

I Almost Made IT!

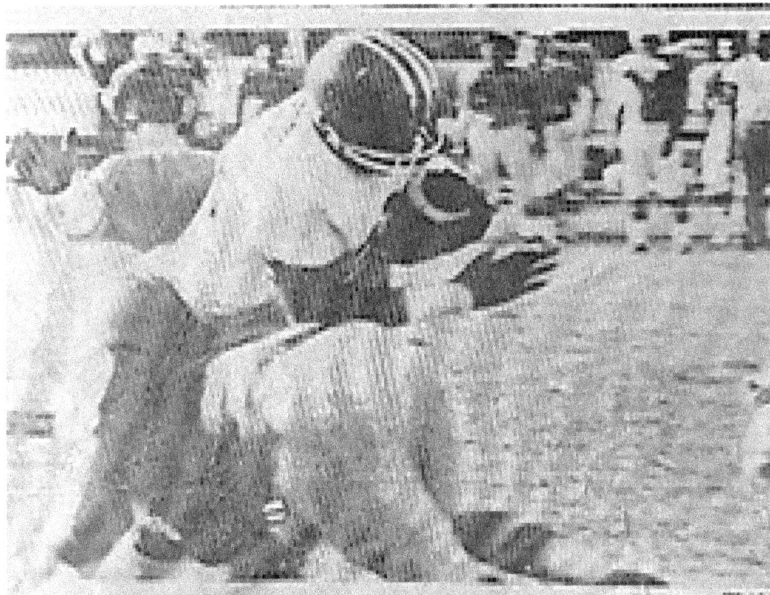

NDS ARE BETTER THAN ONE — DSG running back Sylvester Cash
in trying to break this tackle from a U-Ha defender. He didn't need
win, 34-0.

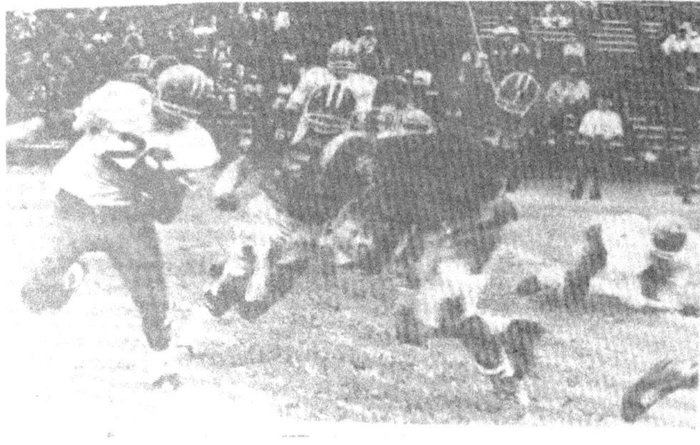

NO PLAC
running b
finds the
blocked b
defenders
Bowl dur
Tourname
team bott
went on to
title, 48-8.

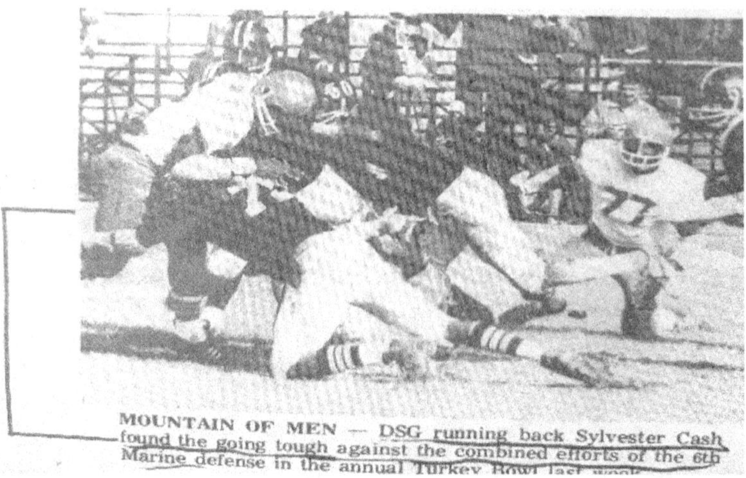

MOUNTAIN OF MEN — DSG running back Sylvester Cash found the going tough against the combined efforts of the 6th Marine defense in the annual Turkey Bowl last week.

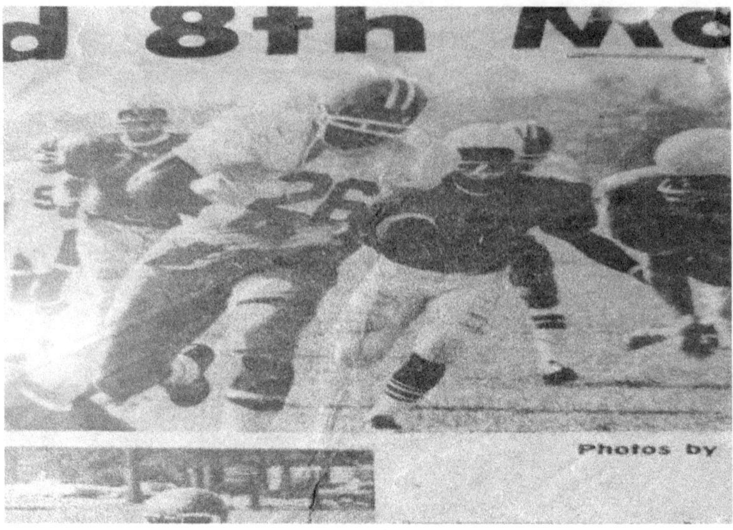

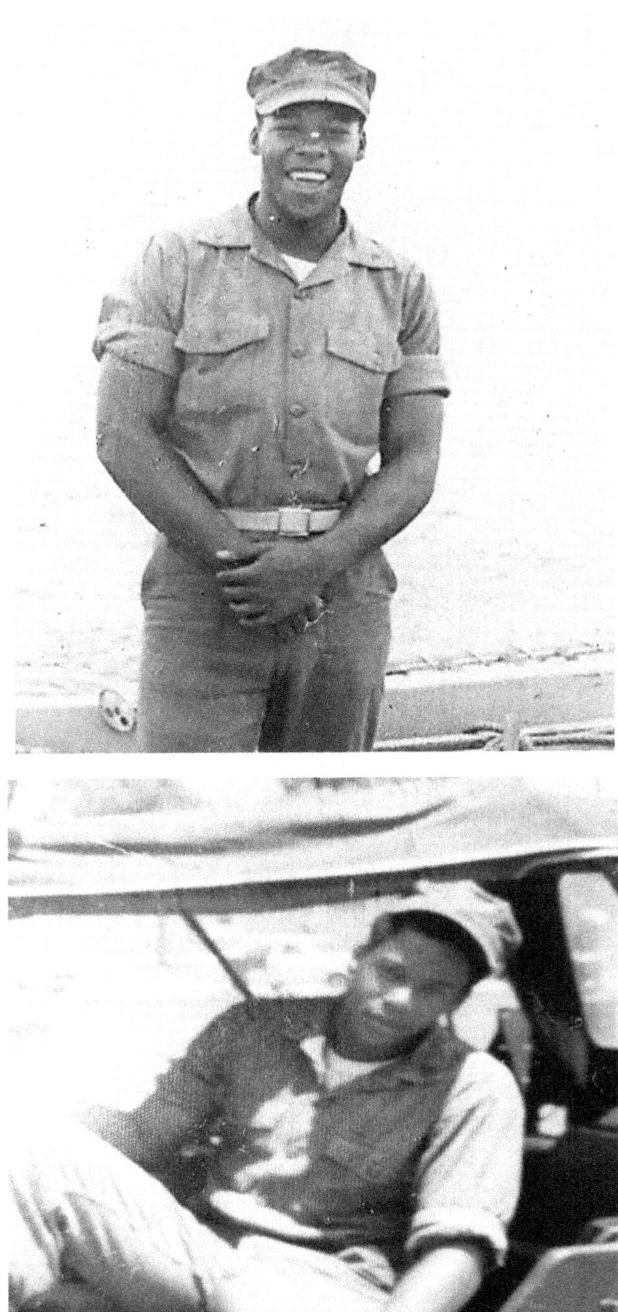

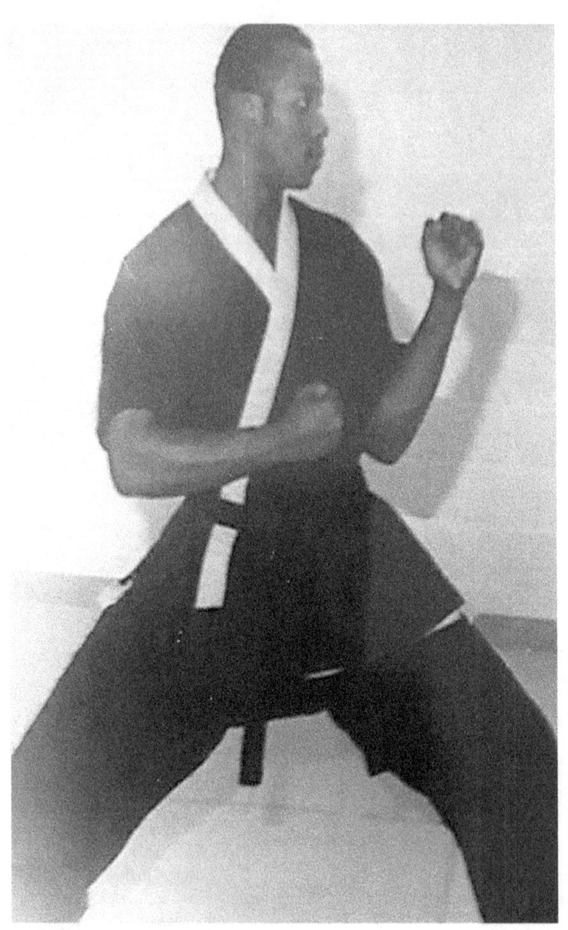

Chapter 4

Martial Arts

Since this book originated because of the relationships, the friendships, and how my life was affected because of karate, I think it is fitting to tell you how it all began.

Now let's first go back to how I got exposed to karate in the beginning. My friend in Junior High, Delonzo Jiggetts, got me into gymnastics. We would go out in the park, right across the street from where we lived on Bryant Avenue and practice tumbling along with two-man stunt routines. Most of them we learned from what we saw in books. Louie, as we called him, was very strong and flexible. I was just strong.

He introduced me to Mr. Douglass Camper, one of the three gym teachers and the gymnastics coach. I would not be paying the proper respect to the other gym teachers that helped me to develop if I did not mention Mr. Powell, who also taught me wrestling.

Mr. Douglass Camper was a man who cared about young people so much that he devoted his life to teaching us gymnastics and taking us around the country to compete.

We had a lot of great talent: Dexter Wise, who became a well-known Minister; Scott, James Randolph, Brian, and Keith Forester; Derrick Camper, Douglass Camper Jr., Delonzo Jiggetts, and Howard, just to name a few I remember. We were from poor families but Mr. Camper found ways to raise funds and get grants to buy uniforms for each of us at no cost to our families. This was my first exposure to organized athletics and competition. We were also required to take karate for discipline and flexibility.

Karate

My first karate instructor was Master Albert Richardson. Master Richardson was an easy-going type of man, but he was also a no-nonsense kind of guy that smiled and was friendly most of the time. He was good at kata, sparring, and Iaido (the art of sword kata). At the karate classes at Lemmel Junior High School and the recreation center where we trained, he was very soft-spoken. But when you went to the regular class at Harlem Park Junior High School, he turned up the exercise.

Every time you would mess up or turn the wrong way during a kata, you had to do 50 push-ups on your knuckles or 50 sit-ups. His students there were sharp as nails and tough. This is when you learned about pain and you stayed because you liked it. I quickly learned the difference between playing karate and learning karate.

I remember an Iaido demonstration that he did for Operation Champ. He cut a watermelon off his student's chest while blindfolded and cut an apple off a student's throat without touching him. The self-defense techniques that he did were so quick and deadly, I was just in awe! These were the greatest things I had ever seen live in real live martial arts.

Master Richardson was killed in a car accident while bringing a group of kids back from a karate tournament in Pennsylvania. He saved them and sacrificed himself! I was about 14 years old and was hoping to go to that tournament, but did not have the money for the entry fee.

I met my next real karate teacher, Leroy Calvie aka Leroy "Superfeet" Taylor, after returning home from a four-year active duty tour in the Marine Corps. Fortunately, by that time, I think I understood life better. What I learned was that if you really want to do something, it is just a matter of pursuing it with passion and having a no-quit attitude. So, let's proceed a bit further and see what happened.

Do you ever wonder what makes a Master? Ever wonder what made your parents much wiser than you? Well, hopefully, you will discover the answers as you continue to live this blessing we call life!

It is written in a lecture in my Masonic ritual:

In youth, we are to occupy our minds with the attainment of useful knowledge. In manhood, we are to apply that knowledge in the service of God and our neighbors so that in age, we are to enjoy the happy reflections consequent of a well-spent life and die in hope of a glorious immortality.

Well, I feel that I have lived long enough now, to understand what this means. At least a little bit better than before! My prayer is that the reader of this will have the opportunity to pursue the meaning and come to understand it, while also living it.

When I was first introduced to karate, I was around twelve or thirteen years old. That was in the 1960s and it was the coolest thing ever. It was also new to our poor community. We had not heard about it in school or anywhere else, just on television.

When I finally found out about it, I was told it was supposed to teach us self-discipline and help us gain our flexibility in gymnastics. All those reasons were fine with me, as long as I could learn to defend myself against the bullies in the ghetto.

I was a White Belt for seven years. You're probably wondering why it took me so long to progress. In Master Richardson's Dojo, you did not get promoted just because you came to class and paid a lot of money. No, you had to learn everything that was required and perform it efficiently and effectively before your classmates.

At that time, your classmates were harder on you than the instructor. Well, I thought that I could beat the system and bounced around from club to club, learning techniques from anybody that looked like they knew karate or could pass themselves off as a Black Belt, so I could get promoted faster. Didn't happen!

Life is the same way: you cannot bypass any phase of growing up to gain knowledge and become an adult. I found myself going around in circles trying to learn karate and, at the same time, trying to figure out life. I was always wanting to be, as my momma used to say, "grown." I thought that I could do anything and everything I thought I was big and bad enough to do, anytime I wanted to do it.

When I was in the Marine Corps, I started to get more serious. I met Michael Pope, from Raleigh, N.C, and we began to train a lot. Mike was quick, fast, and strong.

I was also privileged enough to get exposure from guys that were in Force Recon and UDT. So the exposure I received in the Corps really helped me to get more focused in life and martial arts. I had gotten a better understanding of the basics of karate and life.

After leaving active duty and returning to Baltimore in 1977, I looked for the karate guys I met when I was studying with Master Richardson. I had made a serious decision about karate and my life. That is when I was introduced to Leroy Taylor, who has been my friend and Sensei ever since.

I happened to run into Speedo Brown, whom I remembered from Master Richardson's class as a told him that I wanted to get back into a karate class. After we teenager and talked for a while, he told me that I could go to Fernie's class or a new guy, Leroy's class.

So I remember telling him that I would like to try Leroy's class. I knew nothing about Leroy, but I did remember Fernie Dennis from karate classes before. I did not think I was ready for his class yet. I had flashbacks from Master Richardson's class at Harlem Park.

I remember that first night: I thought that I was in shape. Wrong! We started with 50 four-count jumping jacks, then bends and reaches, push-ups on our knuckles, the edge of our hands, fingertips, and finally wrists. That led to sit-ups, the crocodile crawl, duck walks, wheel barrels, more push-ups, and sit-ups. Then came the punches and kicks!

We did so many punches and kicks that it was unbelievable. We started with singles, then doubles, then triples. After your arms felt like lead weights were on them, you had to do the same thing again with blocks and with a partner. Then came the kicks, never less than twenty-five of each type of kick and off each leg. These kicks were not only kicking to the opponent's legs or waist but kicks to the head and from different stances. I remember not even being able to kick above my waist by the end of the singles, and then he went double and triple kicks? I could barely walk after that first night.

This was just part of the warm-up. Next, we went into katas or forms. We would go through every form from White Belt to Black Belt. At that time, there were about twenty, and Sensei was still creating more katas.

You would keep doing katas until the entire series was completed and then we would go into self-defense. But that did not happen until everyone went back to the level they were at and did all the katas up to the point they dropped out.

Self-defense would include those techniques found in the katas at your level. Sometimes it would involve doing the self-defense while doing the kata to capture all the aspects of the kata and the effectiveness of the self-defense technique. This is called the budo (martial way) or bun-kai (martial application) of the kata. Self-defense was usually fun and interesting. Other times it could be quite painful when someone lost control or was overzealous. So you learned to protect yourself at all times.

After that, we went into what the majority of the class was waiting for: sparring. This is where the better students would shine and the timid students would strengthen mentally and physically. Those that were pretending would be carried off the floor. Not really, but they wished they were taken off the floor!

One-on-one sparring like kata allowed you to show your stuff. When we got to multiple sparring, you got the chance to show your heart. There was no quitting because you got hit too hard or got a bloody nose and or lip.

In those days, parents were not allowed to run on the floor to see if their baby was alright. First of all, that is why they brought their kids down to Murphy Homes Projects-to toughen them up. Sensei would talk to the children in a way that only he could and the tears would dry up and the lion would come out of them. In the end, all would hug, give high fives, and talk about what they did right and wrong. That was one thing that I remember--everyone took care of everyone in the school, especially the children.

When promotion time came up, no one was given a free or easy pass; you had to earn it. In the end, you wore the rank you had proudly earned. I used to watch and listen to the children that had been in class for a while talking to the newer children.

They would encourage them and tell them what they had gone through during their rank test. They would let them know that they were not going to take it easy on them. This was not a threat, but it was to help build their confidence. These children were truly amazing.

I opened my first Karate Dojo at the Parkview Elementary School Recreation Center in 1979 as a Brown Belt. I was blessed that Sensei and Ms. Lin had enough confidence in me to allow me to do this.

This was a big challenge because right down the street was Arnold Mitchell's Karate School. Arnold was known all over. He was one of the most popular martial artists to emerge from the Master Riley Hawkins' Avengers Karate School. Arnold was not only a fierce fighter and competitor, but he was an educator and businessman.

I began by offering classes for free, or at a very low cost for those that could pay. But my school was almost empty. Arnold sat me down one day and gave me a short, to-the-point class on the business of karate.

One of his main points was not to undersell yourself. He said that if you undersold yourself people would think that you had an inferior product or you did not believe in yourself as an instructor. He told me that my students were a lot better than his students, but his classes were full and even though my classes were free or less expensive, I still had very few students. Then he asked WHY?

The only answer I had was because I wanted to do something for the community. He then told me that is all well and good, but you have to understand people, their egos, and the importance of social status!

"People want to go around and brag to their friends, that they take little Johnny or Shanika to karate lessons and I pay x number of dollars per month." People have to impress their friends and colleagues.

Well, I got what he was saying, but being who I am, I never changed the cost. I realized that there was money to be made, but that was not my goal anyway. To me, such is life and I have always been okay with that so Leroy and I never chased the money!

Birth of The Fighting Panthers

In 1979, after all my extra hours of training and teaching, I finally earned my Black Belt. I was so nervous when I got to the seven-on-one sparring portion, I dropped the first guy that attacked me and the others came slower. They eventually overpowered me, but in the end, they knew they had been in a fight. I was Sensei Leroy's first Black Belt. It was an honor of all honors which I still cherish today.

On the karate tournament circuit, I dominated in the Brown and Purple Belt Division until I reached the Black Belt Division. In one of my first Black Belt competitions, I fought a young, extremely gifted young man by the name of LeRoy Hopkins. LeRoy was fresh out of high school and attended the University of Kentucky and was on the wrestling team. I got the first two points on LeRoy, and after then, all I remembered was hearing **Point! Point! Point!** and the match was over.

After that initiation into the Black Belt ranks by LeRoy Hopkins and Garcia Davis, our Senior Instructor Sensei

Greg "Speedo" Brown offered me the opportunity to become an original member of the Baltimore Fighting Panthers Full Contact Karate Team. He came up to me a little while after I was still dazed from a kick and said to me, "You can really take a good punch. How would you like to join this team I am putting together?"

All that was on my mind was this would be a good way of making a little money for the karate school. He was in the process of putting together fighters and was recruiting at local tournaments. Thus, the Baltimore Fighting Panthers was born.

The original team consisted of Leroy "Superfeet" Taylor, John "The Mallet" Taylor, James Boykins, Kenny Bailey, Ronnie Jenkins, Randy Mack, Jerry McKinney, and Sylvester Cash.

I was not the "Iron Man" yet. Later, members were Ronnie James, LeRoy Hopkins, Steave "Awesome" Williams, and Delaney Bolden. I had no idea at that time what was ahead and how it would change my life. I just wanted to help Sensei Leroy by earning a couple of extra dollars to help with the school.

We started that Sunday morning at Champ AC Boxing Gym, located in a small street off West North Avenue near Fulton Avenue. I remember still being dazed from the fight with LeRoy, and with the added alcohol, it was hard making up my mind to get up. But I remember thinking that I did not want to be the only one that did not show up.

The gym was over a garage that painted cars. We had a small boxing ring on the floor, maybe eight feet by eight feet. The ring was composed of small mats on the floor, covered with a canvas cover with ring ropes and turnbuckles.

There was a small kerosene heater that provided an amazing amount of heat in the winter. There was an electric timer that the trainers paid no attention to. Most of the three-minute rounds turned out to be five to ten- minute rounds, but you dared not say anything. If you said anything they would ask, "Are you a fighter or the timekeeper?"

We had stools in two corners, and a couple of chairs lined along the single wall with old fight posters on it. We had an inclined board for sit-ups next to a mirror on the wall; a speed bag across from the door coming into the room; a small storage closet for gloves to hang and a heavy bag in the corner. There was a small dressing room with a padded table; a couple of lockers; a toilet; a shower and a sink.

The foyer area where you came up the stairs was where you would jump rope and do sit-ups and push-ups. Some of the best pugilist competitors that ever came out of Baltimore came from Champ AC. The trainers were Mr. Andrew Singletary, Mr. Bobby, and former, heavyweight contender Mr. Larry Middleton of the Murphy Homes Gym. Notable boxers that came through there during my time included Dexter Harris, a USA Olympic Boxing Team Middleweight; Warren "Chico" Thompson, a USA Olympic Boxing Team Heavyweight; and many more that I cannot remember now.

Many of us worked really hard but were unable to get any long-term funding or sponsors. We were not expected to be around long enough for them to recoup their investments. They did not expect us to be able to compete at the National and International levels.

When we came to the gym to train, the boxers would try to knock us out. I was leery of sparring with them in the beginning. This was supposed to be training, but to them, it was establishing respect and an effort to run us out of the gym.

Most of us as martial artists respected each other and it carried into the ring. Boxers, however, were different and, to me, were animals. I worked with guys that made it known that they did not like us or wanted us in their gym. So when you sparred with them it became a war. That is where we fooled them.

Some of our lightweight fighters would start throwing kicks if they got too rough. When this happened, the boxers would complain that it was not fair! We said we did not complain when they were trying to hurt us, so we just evened it up! Well, things settled down after that.

When I sparred with guys after that first punch, I knew their only goal was to knock me out and I was not going to let that happen. After a few wars with these guys, I gained the nickname "Ironman." I would spar with Chico, who was built like Mike Tyson and he would hit me so fast that I never saw the punch. At the end of our session, he would come over to tell me how well I did that day. Most of the time he would tell me how many times he hit me as compared to the day before.

Speedo would get in the ring with him and it became a war. Speedo only weighed 140 pounds or less and Chico was around two hundred twenty. Speedo would get him so riled up that Chico would start gurgling like a mad dog and try to bite him. They would eventually take off the gloves and go to karate sparring. The outcome would still be the same—Speedo on top.

Speedo Brown worked extremely hard day and night trying to get us fights on the top cards. Speedo could have become a World Champion himself but decided to put his time and talent into us. He spent endless hours on the phone with the top PKA, FFKA, ISKA, and PKC promoters, getting our names out there. He also spent his savings promoting fights locally. He would take us to the Maryland State Penitentiary to spar with the inmates. (You talk about scary.)

The shutting of the steel gates and bob wire fences were frightening enough. But once I got into the ring, they were great to work with. They were much better training partners than the ones outside.

I also fought in back alley garages and backroom bars on boxing cards. I would make sometimes $50 to $100 for a four-rounder. But the gamblers would give me more money for winning.

I once fought in the only Tough Man Contest they ever had in Baltimore. One of my students and good friends, Anthony "Battle Cat" Battle, came to me with a poster he picked up in a liquor store advertising this event and wanted me to train him for it. I looked at it and advised him against it. I told him that we would need about a year to prepare for it.

Because this was open to all comers, he would not only need his heart and novice karate skills, but boxing, wrestling, judo, and grappling training. So I told him to let me go first and then maybe he could go the next time. He agreed. I contacted the promotor, found out the rules, and paid the entry fee. I had already been training to fight Bob Thurman the next month, so I was in pretty good shape.

On the day of the contest, we met with the promoters and the Maryland State Athletic Commission for physicals and to go over the rules. The Commission wanted to shut the event down because they did not want it to become a boxing show. They demanded we kick at least two times a round. Being a kickboxer, that was right up my alley.

The event lasted two evenings. I fought two fights on the first night. My first fight was as a street fighter. This guy drank a half-pint of whiskey and ran into the ring. Well, the fight only lasted about one minute; because I knocked him out.

In my next fight, I fought an old friend and boxer, named Jody Winfield. Jody was a Golden Gloves champion and Olympic prospect, whom I had beaten in a boxing match before. He did not want us to fight the first night. He was not to be taken lightly, but that was the luck of the draw. Jody came out and kicked me right in my groin. I could not complain because it was legal. Well, I kicked Jody all around the ring and outboxed him to win the fight.

I watched most of the competitors and saw some really good fighters. The standout was a boxer. He knocked out everyone that got in the ring with him. The last one he fought they took him out on a stretcher. I remember telling Sensei Leroy, "He is not going to do that to me."

The next night, I fought two more fights before getting to the finals. It ended up being me and the giant boxer. They gave us an option to wear protective headgear and I took it. I came out kicking and he had trouble catching up with me. In the second round, he hit me in the head and made the headgear spin around. Thank God for the headgear!

By the fourth round, he was getting tired and I whispered to him, "Now I am going to knock you out!" He went down a couple of times from the leg kicks and roundhouse kicks. But we went the distance and I came out the victor.

I thought this would be the big one that would get me the endorsements, fame, and movie deals, but all I got was the $3,000 cash prize and the trophy. They never had another competition in the Baltimore area again. **I Almost Made It!**

Full Contact

After a couple more years of fighting on the undercards, the door finally opened up. I was a last-minute substitute on the USA Karate Team competing in three-countries. I had just signed to fight my hometown rival and former stablemate, LeRoy Hopkin. This was a bigger deal for me than fighting LeRoy so I jumped on it.

The team was headed by former Light Heavyweight PKA Full Contact Champion Jeff Smith with the top Karate Point Fighters and Kata experts along with world-rated Full Contact Karate contender. The team included:

- Steve "Nasty" Anderson, #1 U.S. Heavyweight Point Fighter

- Troy Dorsey, U.S. PKA Full Contact Karate Champion

- Tommy Walls, PKA World Contender

- George Chung, #1 Heavyweight Kata

- Charlie Lee, #1 Lightweight Kata, John Longstreet PKA World Contender

- Leroy's younger brother, John "The Mallet" Taylor, was fighting in another part of the United States.

To top it off, they gave Leroy a shot at the vacant PKA Light Welterweight World Title in Canada against Leo Loucks.

We knew that they thought that Leo would beat Leroy, however, he proved them wrong. We all won that night. Leroy won the PKA Light Welterweight World Title and John won the fight that launched him into the PKA Top 10 World Competitor ranks.

In all, I won four tournament point karate fights, and three Full Contact Karate fights in Dublin, Ireland; Birmingham, England. Completing the tour in Paris, France, and knocking out the runner-up of the European Championships. I became the PKA Middleweight Number One World Contender. From that point on, we thought we were finally headed to the top.

You would think we were finally going to make it. As time went on, growing pains developed between Speedo and Leroy. The Baltimore Fighting Panthers and the House of Kat-Sho-Du Karate Club became divided. I tried to stay loyal to both Speedo and Leroy and to act as a facilitator, but I found myself in Leroy's corner.

I don't really know why that happened. I knew he did not need me to survive, but I had come to him in the beginning. Speedo understood and wished us the best. I know it hurt him deeply because he really loved Leroy! He and I still talk and he always shares his knowledge with me. He also helped us when we needed it, whether it was training related, promotions, or martial arts knowledge.

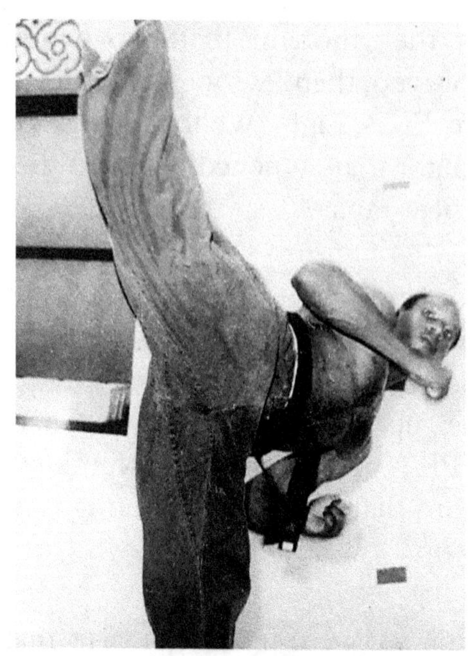

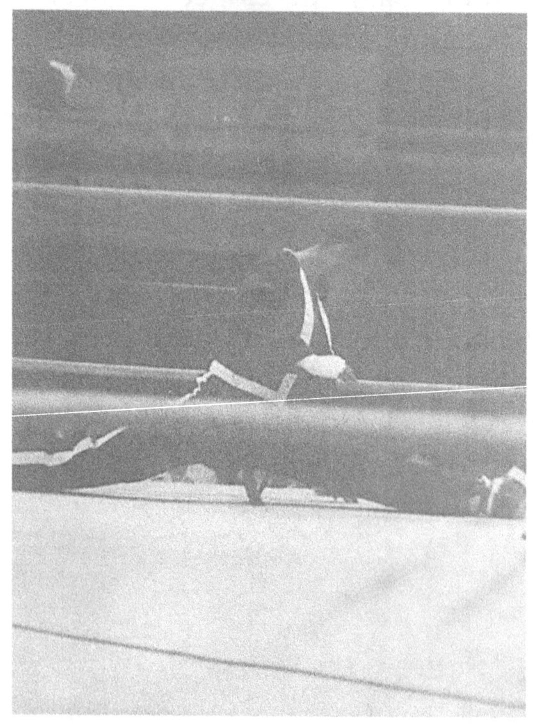

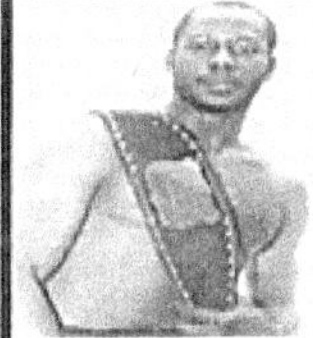
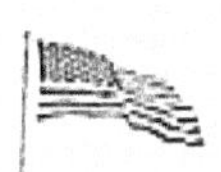

MAIN EVENT
FFKA NORTH AMERIC
TITLE BOUT - 9 ROUN
MIDDLE WEIGHT DIVIS
THE NO. 1 USA MIDDLEWEIGHT CHAMPION
SILVESTER "IRONMAN" CASH
OF BALTIMORE, MD
V S
THE (
Currently the USA Number 1 Champion and Number 1 World Contender in the Middleweight Division, the Iron Man enters the ring tonite on behalf of the United States and goes for the FFKA North American Championship. Training with World Champion Leroy "Superfeet" Taylor, Bunky Herbert, Richard "Trinadazz" Huggins it is quite clear that winning is a way of life and tonite Sylvester maintains that life will go on. Truly a super athletic, from Baltimore, MD welcome the best the United States has to offer the one and only Sylvester "Iron Man" Cash.
Direct from Q
Number 1 Middle
American Cham
boasts a record
titles; 1983 Worl
Championship a
is managed by
professional figh
PURE MOUNTAIN WATER
AREA CODE 215
369-0331
BOXING
MOUNTAIN MEADOW SPRINGS
R.D. #1 • BECHTELSVILLE, PENNSYLVANIA 19505
SANCTIONED MEMBER F.F.K.A.

6

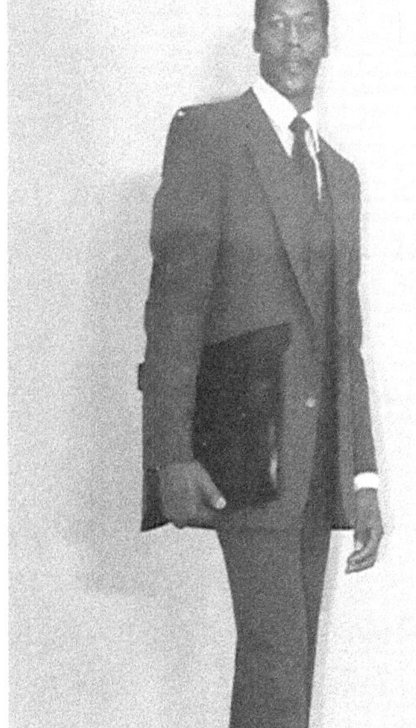

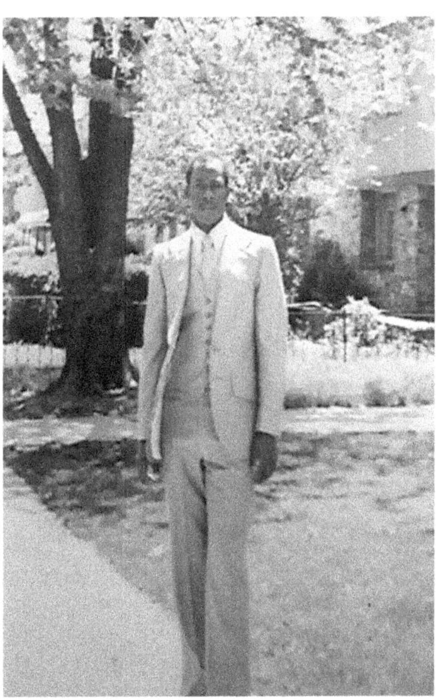

The American Kickboxing Academy

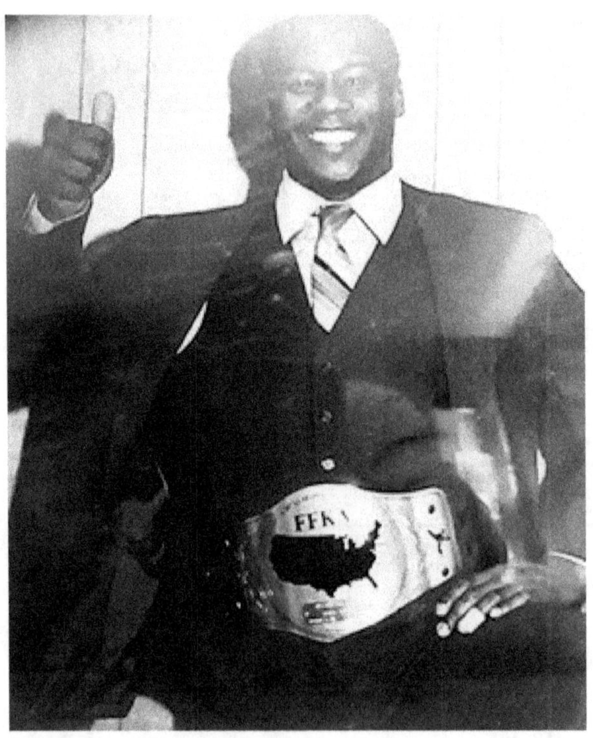

Later, I founded the American Kickboxing Academy in the small community of Pumphrey, located in the county outside of Baltimore City. They had closed down the back portion of the Community Center due to a lack of funding and support.

I met and spoke with the Community Leaders and they allowed me to renovate one side of the closed down area of the building and use it for a small monthly fee/donation. They understood that I had no real money to pay but took me on my word that I would give something to the community. I offered classes in karate, boxing, and kickboxing. Those that lived in the community were only charged half price.

Having finished my Plumbing Apprenticeship, I knew a little bit more about construction and had co-workers and friends in the trades that volunteered their skills and labor for free. You could not ask for better friends. We built a boxing room and an 18x18-foot ring. We put in 150 and 100 lb. heavy bags, speed bags and a double-end bag, focus mitts, striking pads, a jump rope area, sit-up, and pushup area; a carpeted karate and exercise room, and two changing rooms with showers in each.

Special thanks to Chuck Ernest, Jerry Ernest, Charles Owens, Jerry Boorts, John Boring, Bill Beck, and others that contributed their professional skills and labor, material, money, and precious time.

At the American Kickboxing Academy, we produced, worked with, and trained most of the top named competitive karate fighters, Full Contact Karate/ Kickboxing competitors, and boxers in the Baltimore, Washington, and Pennsylvania areas in the mid-1980s and 90s. These included:

- World Champion Leroy "Superfeet" Taylor

- World Champion John "The Mallet" Taylor

- World Champion Eddie Butcher

- United States Champion Steave "Awesome" Williams

- United States Champion Richard "Trinidad" Huggins

- United States Champion Donnie Parker

- United States Champion LeRoy Hopkins

- United States Champion Kenny Bailey

- Top 10 Contenders in most weight classes.

During our time, a championship fight could not be held, on the East Coast especially, without one of our fighters being involved. Still, we were the best of the best! I even got calls to work with fighters that I competed against or would eventually compete against.

One was Rodney "Batman" Baptist, a former PKA U.S. Middleweight Champion. We had been scheduled to fight for his title, but the night before I was scheduled to leave for Canada where the contest was to take place, I received a call from my Trainer "Speedo" Brown that the fight had been canceled because "Batman" had broken his hand in training.

I thought that I was dreaming, that it was a nightmare until I woke up and realized it was true. Well, he knew my reputation as a competitor and a gentleman, so he called me for help in training for his upcoming bout with the World Middle Weight Champion, the "Iceman" Jean-Yves Theriault. However, I had badly injured my hand at a karate tournament the week before, during the Breaking competition, but I still trained with him and was able to give him a good workout. I have always been there to help others and be in shape. He lost the fight but gave it his all!

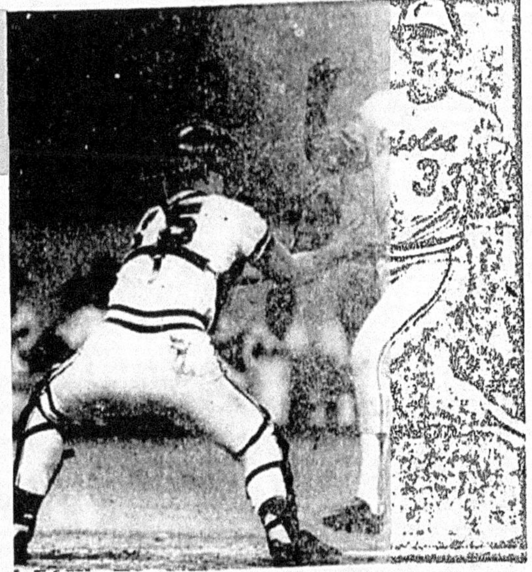

MONTREAL — Sylvester Cash scored an impressive victory here Tuesday night in the Veldrome, defeating Andy Brewer in the feature match of a full - contact professional karate program.

Cash, a Baltimorean, is ranked No. 9 at 169 pounds by world karate standards. Brewer, who hails from Milwaukee, WI, had held No. 10 ranking.

A graduate of Douglass High School and Community College of Baltimore, Cash now attends the University of Baltimore.

He is a member of the Baltimore Fighting Panthers Karate Club, headed by Gregory "Speedo" Brown.

Another member of the Panthers, Leroy Taylor, is scheduled to compete here in October. Taylor is ranked 4th in the world at 147 pounds.

OH NO, NOT EDDIE. — Eddie Murray, normally one of the AL's best baserunners, helped do in the Orioles in Wednesday night's 6 - 5 loss in Minnesota. Failure to slide in an attempt to elude Twins catcher Tim Laudner's tag in this 4th inning action coupled with Benny Ayala's unwise try for second two innings later to run the Birds right out of potential rallies.

Coaching

Life Lessons from Martial Arts

One of my reasons for writing this book is that people I've met along the way who have gotten to know a little about my journey have told me that I should tell my story.

They say I should let people know about the people I've met, the accomplishments I have achieved, and the sacrifices that were made to achieve them. This next topic is for those who are at a point in their life where they are wondering, how do I get to the next level?

Through my formal martial arts training, tournament karate, kickboxing/full-contact karate, and boxing, I have learned so much about what it takes to be successful in life.

For instance, it was really tough losing my shot at the title, but it wasn't the last tough day I had faced that made me want to throw in the towel and quit.

Each day that I am above ground, I may have something interesting happen in my life. Some days may not be as interesting as others or it may be a down day for me. I have days or times when I get lonely or miss people that have been significant in my life. Not to mention when I think about my children, grandchildren, and great-grandchildren! I remind myself that I made the decisions that have led me to this point and I have to live with them and make the best of them.

I read a book a couple of months ago by Evander Holyfield about his life. He said you should always be doing your best in whatever you do, even when you want to quit. I guess I feel the same way. Because of my upbringing and training, I feel stronger now about doing my best and not whining about being treated unfairly. That could probably be a chapter in itself, "The unfairness of the World of Sports as well as in Life."

However, if there have been disappointments and setbacks, there have also been real accomplishments and experiences, and the chance to learn various arts, meet fine people and make friends around the world.

Under Sensei Leroy Taylor's guidance, supervision, and example, I successfully competed locally, nationally, and internationally. With his encouragement and blessing, I have studied other systems and earned a 2nd Degree Black Belt in the Okinawan art of Goju Shorinryu under Master Henry Wilson Jr.

I was twice nominated as Fighter of the Year by Karate Illustrated and Black Belt magazines. I was the first Black Belt from Baltimore to be selected for the United States Karate Team, coached by a former Light Heavyweight World Full Contact Karate Champion.

I also earned a 4th Dahn Master Black Belt, SahBum, in the Korean art of Soobahk under Grand Master Ivanhoe Kim. I was given a Korean name of "KeomJay", which means Silent Warrior and I was only the second Afro-American to reach that level in this Korean Art. Five years after reaching that level, I earned my Shodan in Nishio-Ryu Aikido under Sensei Anthony Tartaglia, 6th Dan, and I had the honor of being presented my certificate and belt by our Japanese Sensei Takao Arisue, 7th Dan, in Japan.

As stated in the title of a book by Rick Pitino, former head coach of the Boston Celtics, "Success is a Choice," your success has to be your choice: you have to choose to succeed at whatever you want to do. In the book, he provides a ten-step plan to help you make that choice:

1. Build your self-esteem

2. Set demanding goals

3. Always be positive

4. Establish good habits

5. Master the art of communication

6. Learn from good role models

7. Thrive on pressure

8. Be ferociously persistent

9. Learn from adversity

10. Survive your own success

To succeed you need a plan of attack. These 10 steps are based upon the premise (that) too many of us constantly undersell ourselves.

We are conditioned to think we can't do things. We are conditioned to settle for less. We are conditioned to think our dreams are always going to be out of reach. We are conditioned to think that it's always going to be other people who grab life's brass ring. We are conditioned to fail. But we don't have to. Instead, we can choose to succeed!

If you find the right teachers and the right training partners for you, martial arts can give you a path so you can choose to succeed every day and keep coming back for more. Your path may not be through martial arts, but understanding what those of us who have followed this path have gone through can help you to understand your own trials and setbacks.

Progressing from a White Belt to the rank of Black Belt is like going from a small child not knowing anything about life to becoming an 18-year-old. At this stage, you may think you have reached the top. WRONG; you have not!

As a first-degree Black Belt, you have reached the stage where all you thought you knew becomes confusing and the path forward becomes even more complicated. The forms get longer, your position in the Dojo becomes more demanding, and your character becomes more important.

You become that person, that Black Belt, that the younger and less experienced students look up to and come to for guidance when Sensei is busy or not around. You are the one they imitate when you are working with them. They expect you to lead and show them the right things to do. They expect you to know all the right answers and to show them how it should be done.

This is the same with life. As you get older and mature, expectations get more demanding. Those in your home, those you come in contact with in your workplace, your school, church, organizations, and community, everyone you touch in your daily life.

As I have traveled in this world, I have found that my training at home, in the military, and Dojo has been my greatest asset. The way I carry myself in the Dojo, the workplace, and in public, lets people know what type of training I have received. It tells them about my character, ethics, work habits, upbringing, commitment, and potential. So remember when you go out that door that you represent so many others that have been involved in your journey in life.

My 1st Certificate from my 1st Karate Tournament given to me by Master Clarence Johnson

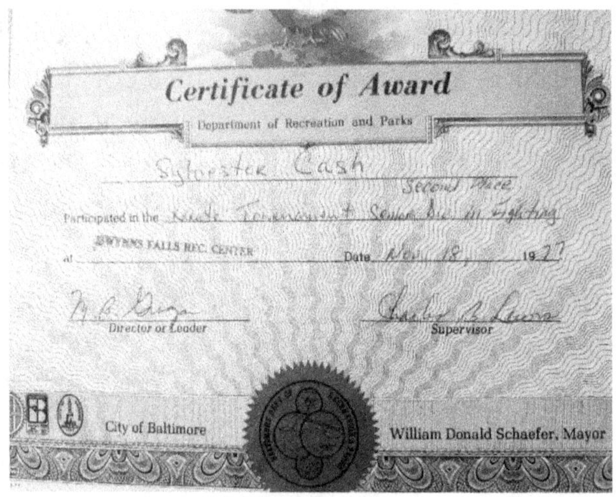

FFKA Middle Weight U.S. Champion

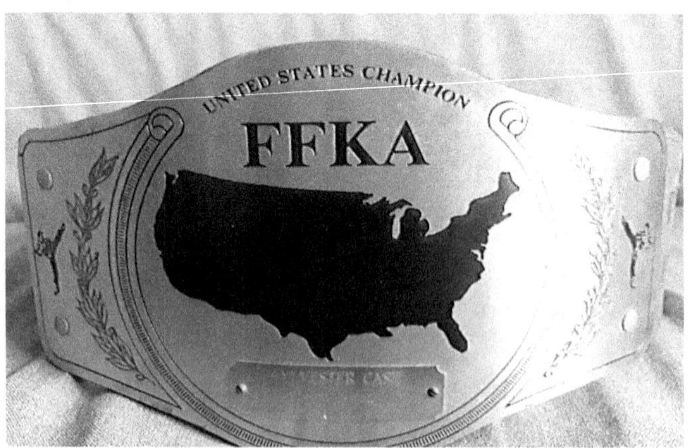

Master Instructor HOUSE OF KAT-SHO-DU

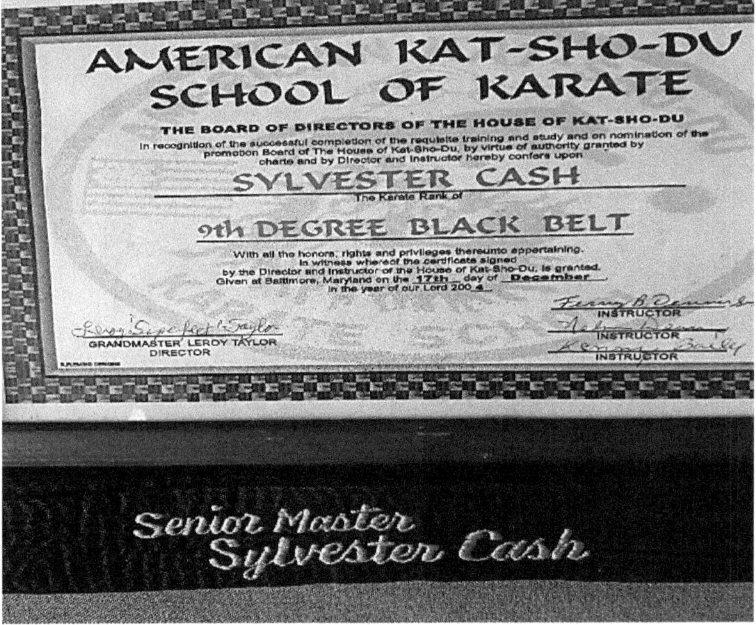

Master Instructor SOOBAHK

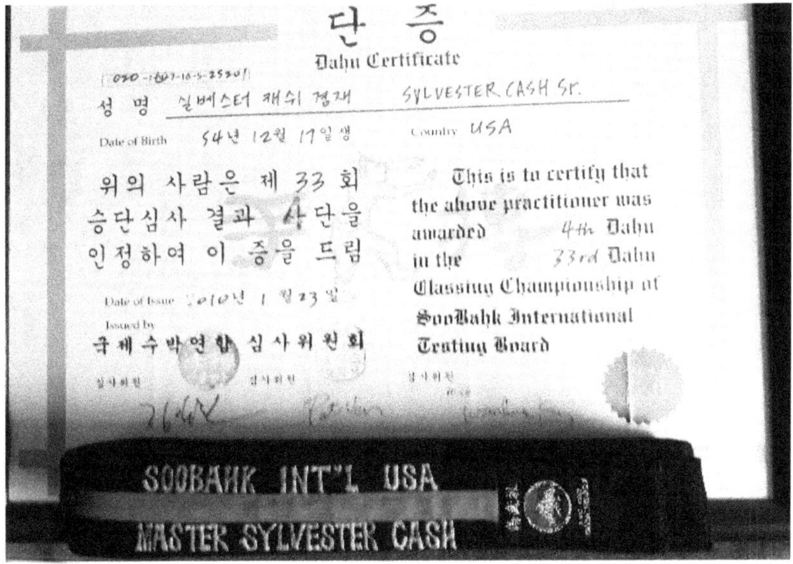

5th Kyu ISSHIN-RYU

Isshin-Ryu Karate-Do

一 心 流 空 手 道

This is to certify that
Sylvester Cash
has successfully completed the course of
instruction prescribed by
Shimabuku Tatsuo Sensei
先生 島袋 龍夫

in Isshin-Ryu Karate-Do,
and is Graded
5th Kyu
in Isshin Kai 一心会 ,
Given at
Bangkok, Thailand
this 10 Day, of February , Year 2012

David McConnell
Chief Instructor
Bangkok Dojo Isshin Kai

2nd Degree Black Belt Okinawan Karate-Do

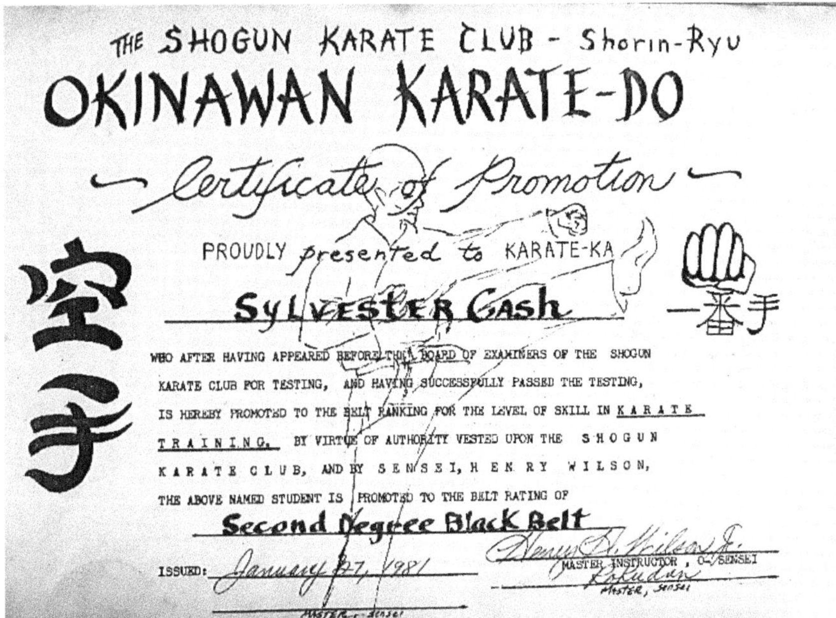

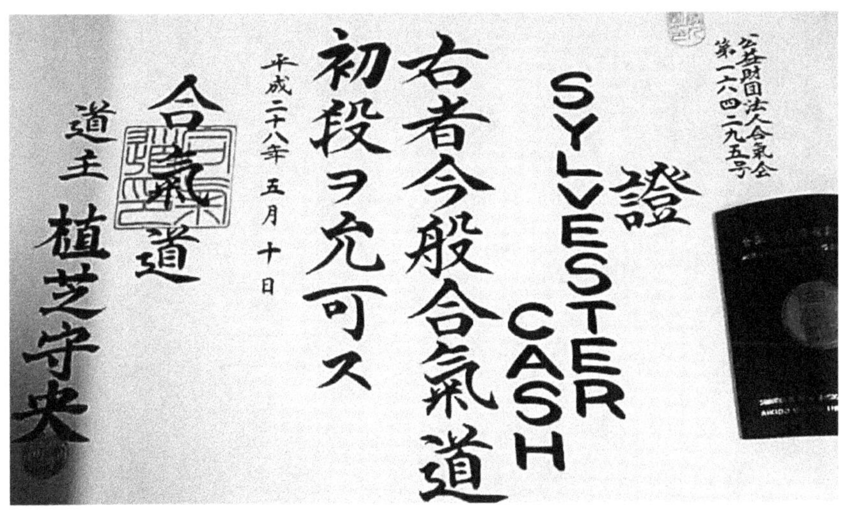

Chapter 4 : Martial Arts

Chapter 5

Masonic Life

Worshipful Master Morning Star Lodge #44 2004-07

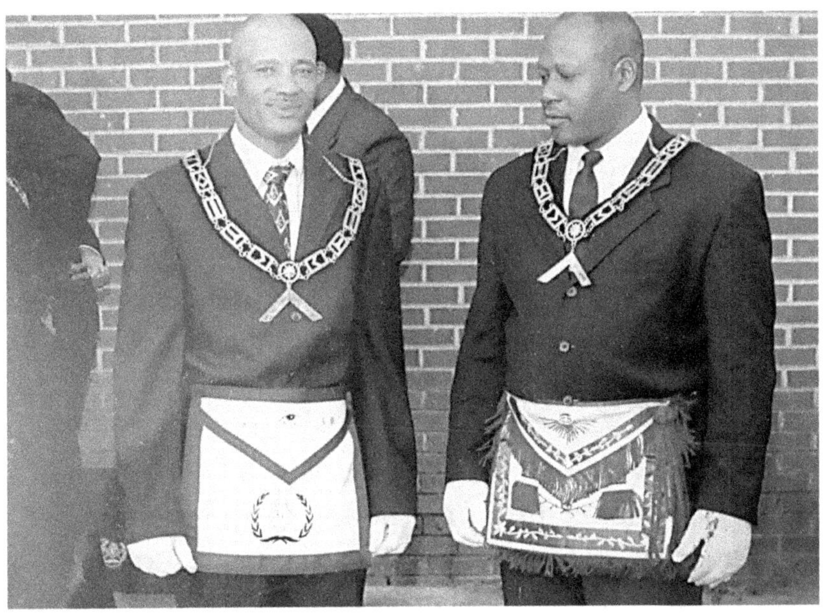

When I first entered college, I planned to become a Physical Education Teacher. After being released from active duty, I had no advanced education or adequate skills to fall back on. I had applied and received a 2nd Class Radio Operators license, which I did not know what to do with.

I thought of becoming an Air Traffic Controller, but I could not see myself working in that type of environment. I could shoot, but I thought, who was hiring shooters or hitmen? I planned to live in Wilmington, North Carolina, but I could not even get a job as a garbage collector. I knew I was in trouble and went back to Baltimore. I knew that I could get my job back in the lumber company because I was still a union member and that was part of the law.

I enrolled in Coppin State Teachers College with plans to major in Physical Education or Accounting after I completed the requirements. To my surprise, after my first year, I was told that they did not offer degrees in Physical Education or Accounting. I then transferred those credits to a junior college,

The Community College of Baltimore. I figured that getting an Associate Degree was better than just having a High School Diploma. My Physical Education Teacher and Accounting plans had changed. I was getting involved with a lot of women so I came up with the bright idea of majoring in the Physical Therapy Assistant Program.

My rationale was "since I enjoyed touching women, I should make money doing it." After my first year in the program I found out that there was a two-year waiting list to get in the program, so I changed my curriculum to general academics.

After graduation, I attended The University of Baltimore, which happened to be a predominately White college. It was there that I learned how uneducated I was. I took almost every class twice. I attended so many tutorial classes that people started to say that I should be able to teach those classes.

I struggled for about seven years there as a D student until my VA Benefits ran out. I could not afford the tuition there, so in what was to be my senior year, I transferred to Morgan State University, a predominately Black college.

I had to complete 24 credits there to graduate, although I only needed 12 credits to graduate. Well, it was cheaper to pay for the 24 credits there than the 12 at The University of Baltimore. At Morgan, I was on the Dean's List every semester and graduated with honors.

The month before graduation, I was notified that the clerical staff could not find grades from a writing requirement and I would not be able to graduate. I pleaded with them to let me walk with my class in 1994 and even threatened to sue them, but they did not budge. I took the course again that summer. Afterward, they informed me that they had found my previous report and apologized. Unfortunately, my momma died in February 1995 and did not get to see me graduate that May.

In my senior year of college at Morgan State University, I took a class called The Black Diaspora about the communities throughout the world created by the descendants of Black African emigrants. I learned of the historical movements of people from Africa, predominantly to the Americas, but also other areas around the globe.

We studied the movement of Africans from freedom into slavery, not only in the United States but also in the Caribbean, Central America, Brazil, and Haiti. I discovered that more than 100 million Africans were taken and dispersed throughout this region of the world.

It was definitely an eye-opener for me since I had just transferred from a predominately white college. There I studied European Culture and Jewish Culture, which were interesting but there was no mention of Black Culture. These studies taught me to understand and respect other cultures. But the Black Diaspora was an eye-opener, exposing me to what our forefathers endured. It actually brought tears to my eyes.

During that class, I had to write a paper on black culture and I chose the topic of the Secret Societies of Africa. During my research, I discovered Freemasonry. This sparked my attention. Later I was talking to my former brother-in-law Rob about it.

He rolled up his shirtsleeve and said, "You want to know about this." I almost fell out of my chair! He had a big Masonic tattoo on his shoulder. I was impressed! We talked a little while longer and then he said, "Come with me. I want you to meet someone."

Well, he took me to meet no other than Mr. Willie R. Montgomery. Once again, I almost fell over. I had known the man I called Mr. Montgomery for over 10 years at work. I tell people that he was such a hard worker and knew so well how to get things done that they had to hire five people to do his job when he retired from government service. One of the first questions that they ask you during your investigation is "Why do you want to be a Mason?"

Well, just like 98% of those asked this question, I too could not put it into words. But what I did know is that when I knew Mr. Montgomery was a part of this organization, there was no doubt in my mind that I wanted to be right beside him.

Mr. Montgomery was a giant of a man. He stood about 6 feet 5 inches, and he seemed to have the biggest hands in the world. One of his hands seemed to cover your whole chest!

He was not only big in stature but he also had a big heart and personality to match. He would do all he could to get the job completed and to please everyone involved.

Once I got my 1st Degree, Mr. Montgomery introduced me around at work and I discovered that Freemasonry was all around me. I had Brothers working in the same office and even right next to me and never knew it.

After I completed my training and became a Master Mason, I would watch and listen to the way Mr. Montgomery handled situations and events. I watched him handle four or five situations at a time and never broke a sweat. I used to ask him how he got so many things done in so little time. He never gave me an answer.

When we had our Master Mason Ball and other events, we would have from 500 to 1,000 guests, and Mr. Montgomery would do the floor plan. He knew who could sit at whose table, who would talk to whom, and what they liked to drink and eat. He knew the types of rooms our guests wanted and would pay for, what type of entertainment they enjoyed and would support, and who would be late paying their bills.

Brother Past Master Mr. Willie R. Montgomery

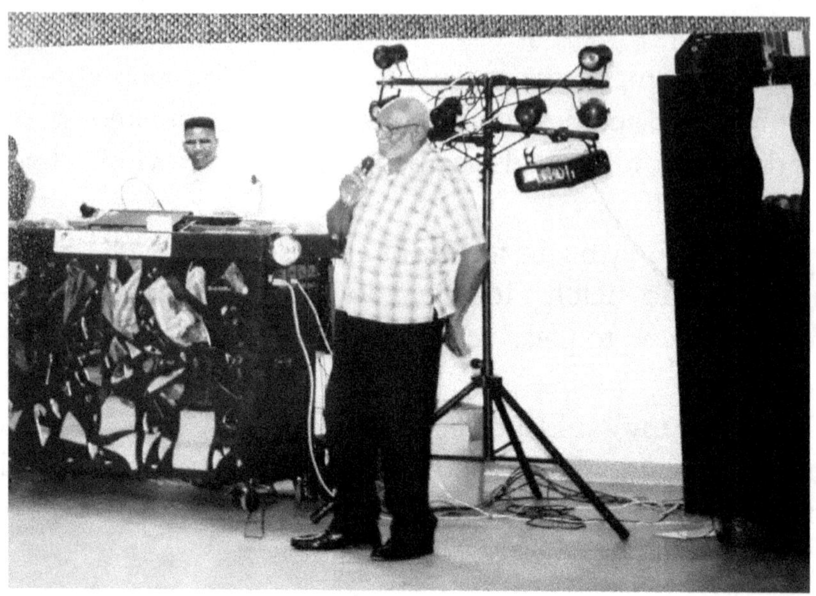

My lodge, Morning Star #44, would travel every year to North Carolina, Connecticut, Washington D.C., and Virginia to participate in their degree work and fellowship with our Masonic Brothers and Sisters from other Masonic houses, families, and friends.

Mr. Montgomery knew what each person on the bus ate and drank, but first, he made sure that the Worshipful Master was taken care of. If he did not teach me anything else, it was that you always take care of the Head of your organization. It did not matter what you felt about him or his policies, the Craft voted him in so you should support him.

He knew who needed to sit next to whom, who should sit in the front of the bus, and who should be in the back of the bus. He would have us systematically load and unload the bus. He was an amazing man.

The last time I saw him he apologized for never answering my question about how do you get so many things done. But I found the secret by watching and listening. I learned by participating and serving others.

I sat as the Worshipful Master three consecutive years, 2004-2007, and he was there to whisper words of wisdom in my ear and support my endeavors. I sat not because I wanted to, but events in the Lodge prevented me from leaving the East until we had someone prepared to ascend to the East. So I remained in office until my Wardens were officially qualified to hold that office and, the entire time, he supported and encouraged me.

During a few times when I was deployed abroad—to Germany during 9/11, Qatar, during Iraqi Freedom, etc.—I would call to ask him to take care of things with my family and it was taken care of. Other times, just to hear a friendly voice, I called him and he would be on the other end with words of encouragement and friendship. Just like many others, I miss him, but God needed him more."

These days I find myself busy just like him, with a kitchen table full of papers, receipts, phone numbers, and Lodge work. I am talking to Brothers and their significant others about solutions, not problems.

I am willing to travel to help and teach a Brother or anyone else that may just need a little boost or hand of friendship and brotherly love. I am trying to keep the lodge business flowing and observe the will and pleasure of the Worshipful Master, always studying, training, and teaching Masonic rituals and usages. Because God brought him and many others like him into my life, I am proud to be a servant to my family, my fellow man, my Craft, my Worshipful Master, my brothers, and first in my life, my God.

There are not as many men knocking down the doors to join Freemasonry as in the early years when life was much more difficult. As when our community was in dire need of a support organization with influential and powerful black men involved. Like when we only had the Church to lean on for protection and as a sanctuary. What people do not realize or care to understand is the Craft is a unique organization.

Even though we are a volunteer organization and we vote on issues, we are not a democracy. Prince Hall Masonry is the oldest Fraternal Organization in our community. It exists because we are founded on principles and practices that we care not to change to keep up with modern practices as others have.

Our purpose, goal, and mission are to help better our world through charity and mentoring. We are not a religious organization, but our teachings are biblically based. We are not a secret organization, but "an organization that has secrets." I am told that the Greek fraternities have tried to model themselves after us. There have been a lot of great men that rose from the rank and files of Freemasonry to contribute and impact our nation's history as well as world history.

I tell those that endeavor to join our Craft the same thing that I was told, "You only get out of it what you put in it." Most of them, I don't think really get it or understand what that means. Others are so biased on what they are trying to personally obtain from becoming a member that they just choose not to hear it.

I spend a lot of time trying to explain Masonry and the concepts but it still only comes down to what you do in the organization. In the study classes for the Ancient Craft Degrees, I cover the symbolism and the charges which tell you specifically what you are supposed to do within your private life, within the community that you live in, and in the outside world. As a reminder, I also explain to them how those things are represented in our daily lives.

We learn that "As you increase in knowledge you will improve in social intercourse." I can stand as a witness to the validity of this statement. I am an introvert by nature and all of my life I have been limited in my conversations. I believe that I should not say anything unless I have something to say. I have been around people all of my life that just talk, talk, talk, and they are not talking about anything of interest or that anyone else cares about.

I always felt that I was limited in my knowledge of life and subjects of interesting social conversations, so my social interactions were few. I also used alcohol as a method to start talking. That way if I said anything improper or stupid, I could blame it on the alcohol. I remember in grad school sitting in class listening to one of my classmates rambling on about things that had nothing to do with what we were discussing in class and he received an A for that class.

I, on the other hand, spent hours and hours trying to understand the course material and only contributed when I was called upon and I received a B.

I went to one of my professors, who also happened to be my advisor, to discuss this issue that I felt was unfair. He sat me down and explained to me how the system worked. He told me that, in essence, it did not matter what you say, you just had to have an opinion. You also had to talk! So I received a B, which is the lowest grade you can get in grad school because I would not talk.

I could not afford to fail a class that the U.S. Government was paying for. Those classes were $1,000 each. If you failed a class, you had to pay the money back. After that conversation, I began to talk about anything and always volunteered to do whatever task the professor needed to be done.

Masonry helped me, not only to improve my study habits but to have more confidence in myself as a public speaker. After a while, I could not wait to share what I had learned with other Brothers. I had a speaking part on every degree team. I started performing the longer lectures and eventually the two longest lectures the Middle Chamber and the Masonic Burial.

Once, I became proficient and certified in those two, I became well known among the Craft. Not every Lodge had someone proficient in these or comfortable speaking in public. So when a Lodge needed them performed, I was one of the Brothers that they called.

I started receiving free tickets to affairs for doing the Middle Chamber and got paid to perform the Masonic Burial. I love to talk to those seeking light in Masonry. I have seen a lot of Brothers shy away from it. When you are doing something that you enjoy, you don't mind doing it. I can talk to people for hours about Masonry.

After many years of meetings and discussions, The Grand Lodge of Maryland A.F.&M and The Most Worshipful Prince Hall Grand Lodge of Maryland and Its Jurisdiction, A.F.& M, signed a Mutual Agreement of Recognition.

This was a historical event for both organizations and the Grand Masters decided to do a "Joint Raising" to be held at the Grand Lodge of Maryland located in Hunt Valley. This was a first, in their state-of-the-art facility. Most of us had never seen anything like this before. They owned all the land and the buildings on it. They have a building for every Masonic House. They even have Masonic Homes Community.

When the terms were finally set for the Joint Raising, notices were sent out to each Lodge to participate in the event. There were fewer than we expected that came out to audition for parts. I immediately put my name in to be the Worshipful Master of the Degree, along with my Senior Warden, Junior Warden, and Senior Deacon. So, Morning Star Lodge #44 dominated the major parts of the degree.

The other lodge Worshipful Masters knew coming in that they could not complete with me so they did not even attempt to try to get that part. However, one of the Worshipful Master really wanted to be a part of this event, so I agreed to let him do the first half of the degree and I would do the second half, the major section.

The degree was "off the chain." They had never seen a *Raising* done like we performed it and were mesmerized. We made Prince Hall Masonry proud and we were the talk of Masonry on the entire East Coast. I was the first Prince Hall, Worshipful Master with my Wardens, and Senior Deacon to seat in their East.

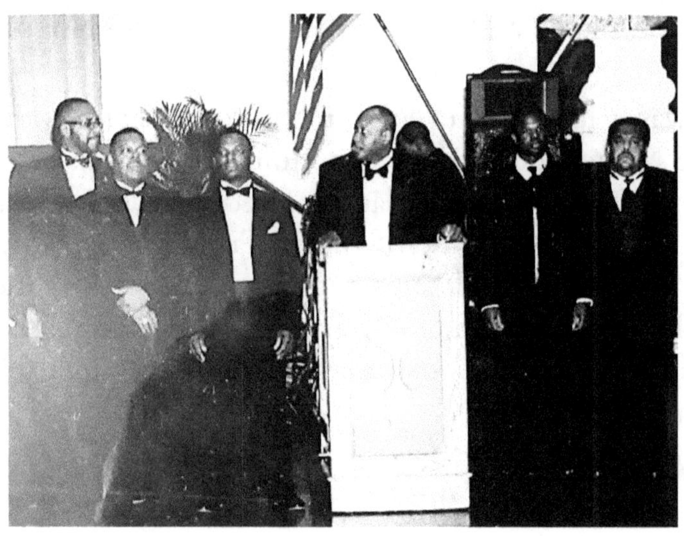

After leaving the Oriental Chair, I was immediately deployed to Seoul, South Korea, to assist in the negotiations for the Yongsan Relocation Project. Our Past Grand Master, the late, Honorable Shelton D. Redden, appointed me District Deputy Grand Master At-Large Korea in recognition of the work I had done during my terms as Worshipful Master. I knew neither what this meant nor what my responsibilities were. It was later explained to me that I was overall the District Deputy Grand Master in Asia from the Maryland Jurisdiction.

Grand Master Redden wrote a letter to the foreign jurisdictions informing them that I was his representative and was to be given all honors that were to be given to him. However, I never presented myself that way to the Brothers. There in Seoul, I met Brothers from Oklahoma, Texas, and Washington State.

I began to attend meetings there and doing degree work with them. I fit right in. I attended the Far East District Sessions and met Brothers from the Philippines, Guam, Okinawa, Mainland Japan, and Europe. I remember saying to myself, "This is what Masonry is all about."

After Grand Master Redden left office, I confronted the new Grand Master, the Honorable Melvin Thorpe, and explained to him that I had never been given any marching orders. He said to me, "I don't have to because you are already doing what you should be doing." He told me, "I have heard all about what you have been doing out there! You are doing good things and it makes Maryland look great. Keep it up!" This was an honor and joy to hear! I always say, "Let my work speak for me."

After retiring, I decided to stay in Thailand. I had been working and fellowshipping with Siam Military Lodge #30 in Bangkok, who are under the Jurisdiction of Delaware, for a least four years so I decided to demit to them.

It was a hard thing to do, but I had been working with them and educating their Brothers all of that time. At the time of this writing, I have taught and raised over 26 of the 34 Brothers on their rolls. I was elected as Secretary of the

Lodge and appointed District Grand Lecturer by the Grand Master, the Honorable Issace Morris.

Being the Secretary of the Lodge is probably the most important and tedious position there. It takes a lot of understanding, communication, patience, and research to keep up with everything going on in the Lodge. You have to be on top of the Grand Lodge Constitution, the Lodge's by-laws, and any other communications coming from the Grand Lodge while keeping the Worshipful Master abreast of what he needs to know before he needs to know it. You are also responsible for keeping the Lodge informed of what the Worshipful Master and the Grand Lodge want them to know.

As the Grand Lecturer, you have to be proficient in the Rituals and Lectures. You must be able to explain the workings of the Lodge and Grand Lodge. You have to understand each Brother's position, role and responsibilities, and be ready to assist them in their time of need. In this position, you need to be up on protocol and procedures at the Grand Lodge level, and see that the Lodge is proficient in its execution when required. Like all organizations, those that have been there for a while don't like change, even if the change follows the regulations and law of Prince Hall Masonry.

I was Elevated to 32nd Degree Sublime Prince in 2001 to Hiram Consistory #2 in the Valley of Baltimore. A few months later, I petitioned Jerusalem Temple #4 to become a Shriner and was created as a Noble of the Ancient Egyptian Arabic Order Noble Mystic Shrine.

I did not participate much in these houses because not only did I not have the time, but I joined for the wrong reasons. I got into a discussion with my ex-wife one day concerning Masonry. I gave her the correct answer but she disputed it and said that a friend of hers, who was a 33rd Degree Mason, had said something different from what I told her.

In frustration, I told her that because he was a 33rd and I was still a 3rd Degree Mason that did not mean he was right. So, from that point, I felt that unless you had the numbers, people would not listen to you.

So, I went after the numbers with a couple of my Cable tows. We went for a few weekends from 06:00 to 18:00 two days each weekend. We walked, sang, and prayed. So all Masons can pray! In the last weekend section, our Lodge had an affair that lasted until 02:00 and we had to be at the Lodge at 06:00.

Brother Crawley was in-charge of the affair, so he did not get to bed until almost 0400a.m. Well, low and behold he was not there when we started our last degrees. They were going to start without him and that meant he would be dropped from the class and have to start all over again the next year. I overheard what they were planning to do, so I knew that they could stop you from talking and singing, but they could not stop you from praying.

One of the Brothers got to a phone and called and woke him up. Before we start anything we always start with prayer. So knowing that once we started after the prayer he would be taken out of the class, I did the prayer. I prayed for one and a half hours, with the other Brothers joining in with songs until he got there on the line with us. It was nothing they could do to him because we had not started yet.

When I did go to a Consistory meeting, I did not participate, I just became a seated member/a "wallflower." I feel that Brothers who do this become more of a burden on the lodge than an asset. The thing is, Do They Realize It? The Body brings them into the organization expecting them to be an active working Brother, not just a "Card Carrier."

Each organization has officers with responsibilities and duties. These positions are manned by Brothers elected and appointed each year. Most of the time, they are recommended and nominated to advance based on merit. But you also find in smaller lodges that they are in an officer position because there was no one else at the elections that wanted or could hold the seat. That is when you know your Lodge has problems.

Since I retired, I have not only demitted out of my mother lodge Morning Star Lodge #44 into Siam Military Lodge of the Delaware Jurisdiction, but I have moved my membership from the Consistory, Hiram Consistory #2nd Shrine, Jerusalem Temple #4 in Baltimore to Joseph I. Staton Consistory #103 and Amenophis Temple #217, both in Angeles City, Philippines. I am glad to say that I am still an Honorary Member of Morning Star Lodge #44 and was told I would be nominated to be Honorary in J4 also.

I have become active in each house and I don't feel like a fly on the wall anymore. I am constantly learning and teaching what I am learning to others in these houses.

I completed the Orient of the Far East Masonic Academy College of Morals and Dogma. This certification allows me to instruct and lecture on the 29 other degrees of Masonry. In 2018, I was selected as Sublime Prince of the Year and nominated to receive the Honorary 33rd Degree, the last degree in Masonry, for all that I have accomplished and contributed. I am also learning and teaching in the Temple and was selected as Noble of the Quarter.

I was elected President of the Masonic youth group, John E. Peterson Council #5, of the Knights of Pythagoras. This group is for the youth ages 8-20. They are Filipinos and most speak English as well. They are very smart. Most come from single-family homes, whose income is very, very low by American standards. Some just come to get a filling meal. We teach them how to hold a structured meeting, we talk about their goals and dreams, do small projects to allow them to show their skills and talents, and we take them on educational and recreational trips.

District Deputy Grand Master At-Large South Korea

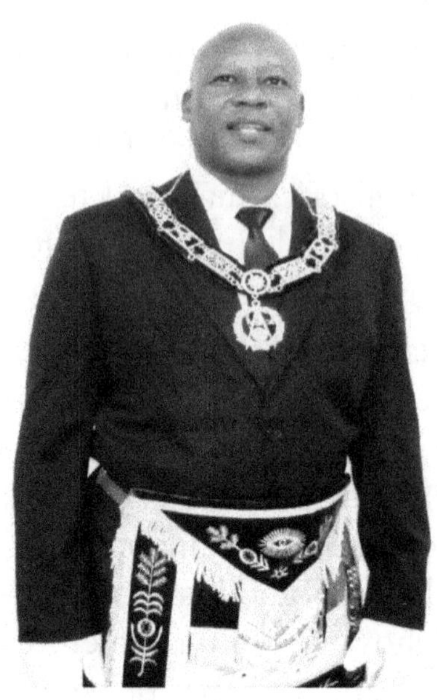

District Grand Lecturer Delaware District 4 Delaware

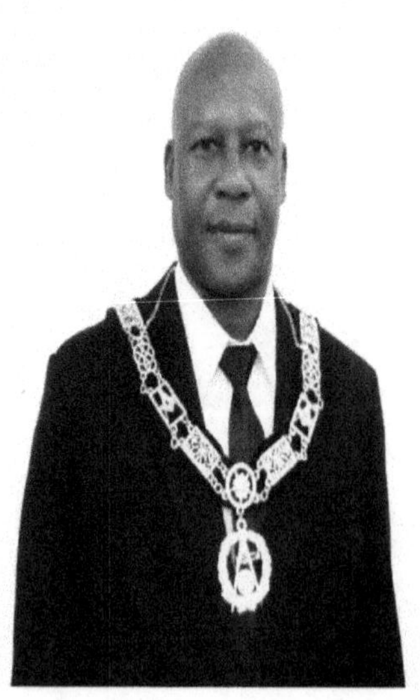

Sublime Prince of the Royal Secret 32nd Degree Hiram

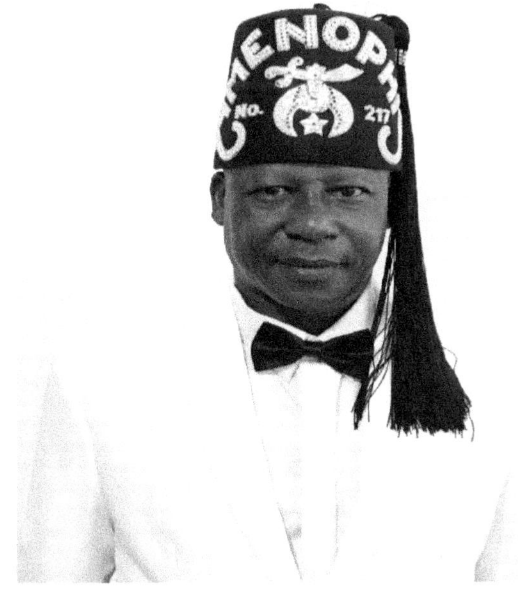

Consistory #2/ Joseph I. Staton #103 33rd Degree Class 2020

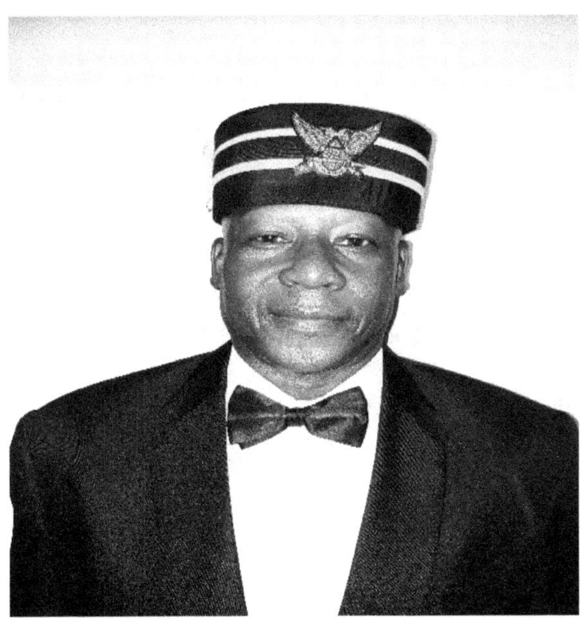

Jerusalem Temple #4 Baltimore, Maryland/ Amenophis Temple #217 Philippines

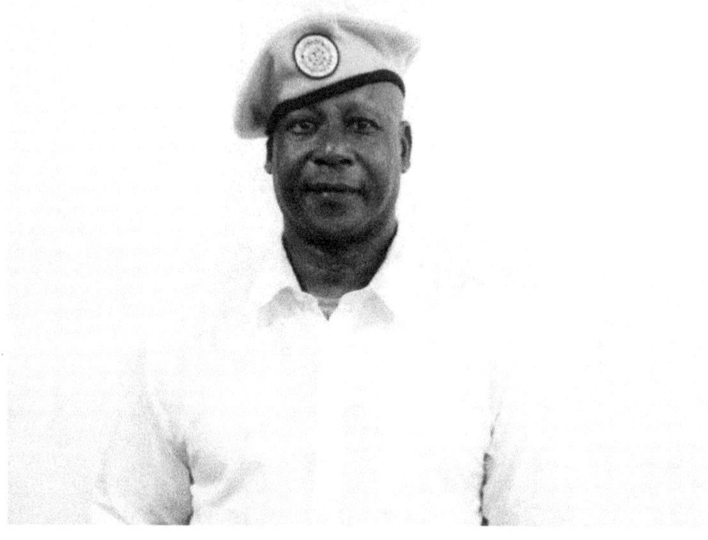

President John E. Peterson Council #5
Order of the Knights of Pythagoras

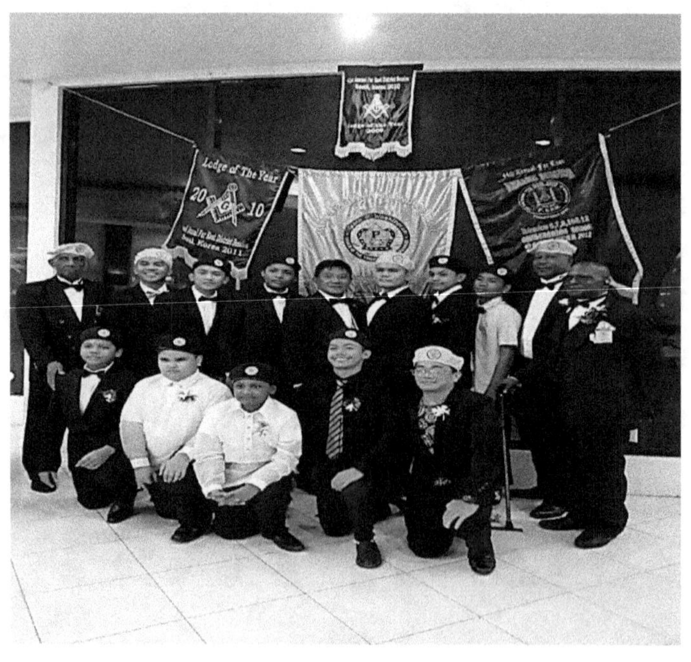

JOHN E. PETERSON COUNCIL#5
KNIGHTS OF PYTHAGORAS

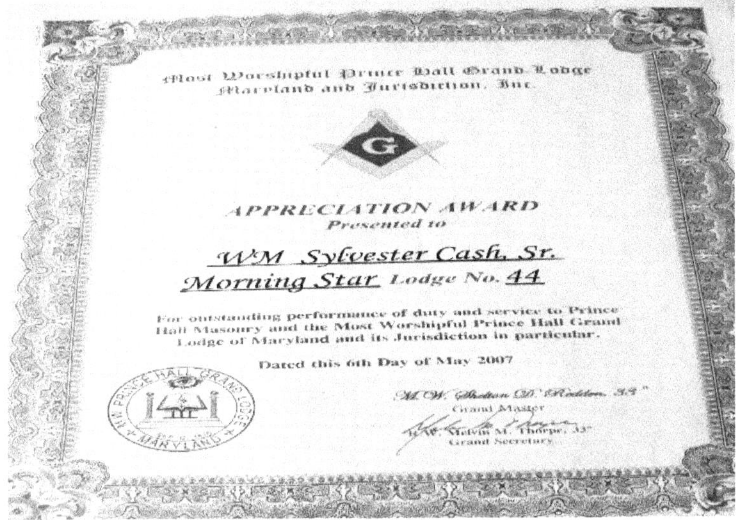

Sublime Prince of the Year 2018

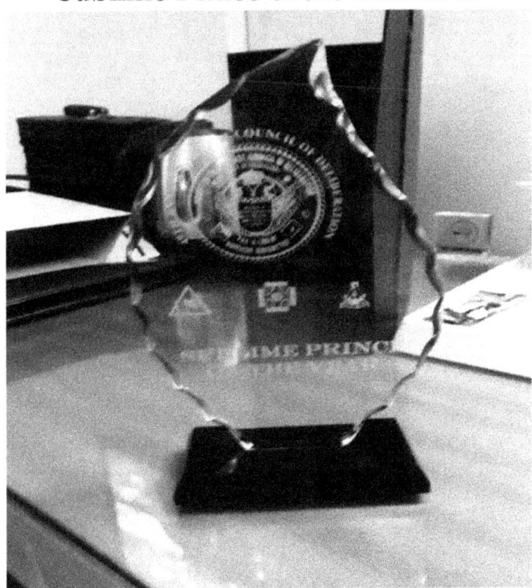

Noble of the Quarter 2019

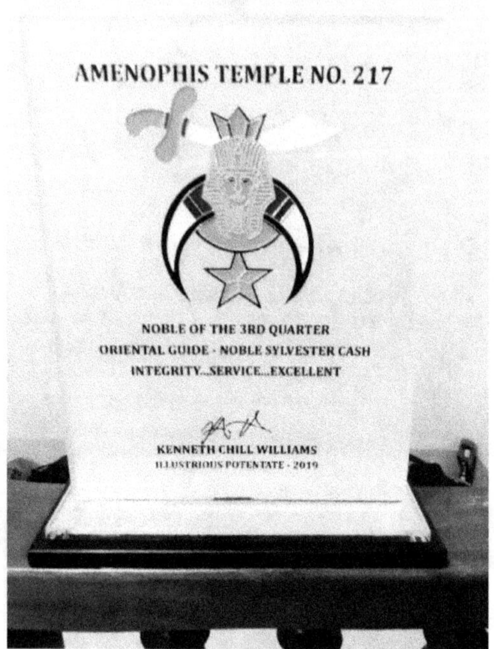

Chapter 6

Work and Career

Childhood Work-Life

As a child, around nine years old, I started to take little jobs around the neighborhood. The first one, I still remember, was working in Mr. Boone's Grocery store, stocking the shelves, and taking out the trash.

Mr. Boone was kind to my mother and the people in our neighborhood, giving them food and groceries on credit until they received their welfare check on the 1st of the month. When I was around 11 years old, I got my second job delivering newspapers around the neighborhood every afternoon after school and on Saturday and Sunday mornings. The newspaper men, I do not remember what they were called, would come to your house and tell you that you could make about $30-$100 per month depending on the size of your route and if everybody paid their bill on time (which rarely happened). That kind of money never evolved, if anything, I always owed them.

Then, when I was around 15 years old, I would get up at 2:00 a.m. to get to the Cloverland Milk Dairy at 3:00 a.m. The strategy was to get there before most of the other boys so you could get a job that day. I would work on the milk truck delivering milk to homes and stores till about 11:00 a.m. I would make about $10-$12 and get to eat day-old doughnuts and drink milk and juice for free. I would give my money to my mother to help buy food for the house, but she would tell me to save my money to buy clothes.

I was fortunate to have acquired a good work ethic at an early age. I used to watch my cousin Darryl Moore, "Pughy", working, doing chores around the house like washing dishes. He was about a year younger than me.

Even though I was the oldest, everything he did I wanted to do. I remember seeing him wash dishes so I started washing dishes. After that first time, I found myself washing dishes and cleaning the bathroom all the time. Then, one summer, he went to my grandparents' house in North Carolina to pick tobacco. But I will tell you about that after I tell you this.

Since my work ethic was better than average, Social Services got me a summer job working for the Social Security Administration at the Paca & Pratt Building. This program placed inner-city youth from low-income homes in work settings for the summer. The program was to give them work experience and a chance to earn a little money.

I went down and got my social security card and a work permit and I was all set. I reported to work the first day with a shirt and tie on. I was very shy and uncomfortable. I knew everybody knew that my family was on welfare or I would not be in the summer program. But, to my surprise, nobody ever said anything about it. There were women everywhere and the sound of laughter and chatter throughout the day. I had never been around that many women who were not family in all my life. Then I found out that my cousin Louise worked there, which made things more comfortable.

I worked as an Assistant File Clerk. I learned to file folders, research and retrieve files, and how to type a little. I never tried to flirt with the ladies; not because I was so much younger but because I did not have a clue on what to say or do.

The work was not hard at all and I remember thinking to myself, "This office work is not for me. I need to be doing manly-type work. I need to be getting dirty and sweaty." A year later, while picking tobacco and again while lying in the muddy fields and jungles, that mindset changed.

Junior High School is where I met another man that helped me change my life—Mr. Doug Camper. He not only coached the Gymnastics Team, but he also took us to meets on the weekends and got us to volunteer and paid summer jobs with Operation Champ. Operation Champ was a recreational program put together for inner-city kids.

They provided games, karate, baseball, basketball, gymnastics, and weightlifting at recreation centers throughout the inner city of Baltimore. They also had trucks that would go out during the summer to neighborhoods and set up the gymnastics equipment—trampolines, tumbling mats, balance beams, side horse, and parallel bars along with other sports apparatus. We would teach and give demonstrations. In the evening they would provide musical entertainment with local bands and singers. They would also provide food, sodas, milk, and juice for free during the day and hot dogs and soda in the evening. Those were the days!

I was on the gymnastics team and just entering high school and only 15 years old, but you needed to be 16 years old to work as a paid employee. I started out doing volunteer work, teaching gymnastics as a recreation aide with this program. Doing this volunteer work, assured me a paying job the next year.

That was when I discovered what real work was. My cousin Pughy started telling me how much money he was making picking tobacco at my grandfather's house in North Carolina, so I decided once again to go do what he was doing. I left my volunteer job with Operation Champ and went down to my grandfather's house to pick tobacco.

Well, we started on Monday at 03:00 a.m. We had breakfast, which consisted of eggs, chicken, biscuits, and preserves. At around 04:00 a.m., we got on the back of Grandpa's truck and went down the road. We arrived at the field before daybreak and began work.

My grandmother showed me how to pick the leaves off the stalk. Pretty easy to do, you might say. What you do is with your right hand reversed, pointing your thumb down to the ground and rotating your arm and hand clockwise around the stalk, grab all the leaves. Once you have taken all the leaves off the stalk, place them under your left armpit and then shuffle over to the next stalk.

Again, pretty easy, you say? Oh, did I mention that the stalks were only about four inches apart, only about four inches off the ground and that we were only on the bottom of the stalk? So, you are bent over the entire time until you take what you have and put it in the cart.

This particular morning started hot humid and the bugs were busy biting you, flying in your ears, mouth, nose, eyes, and any other place they could fly into! As the morning went on, it began to rain. I thought we would be taking a break until it stopped. WRONG! We kept right on working through the rain. After the rain, it got even hotter and the sap from the tobacco leaves began to form a layer of skin over me. The bugs began to really attack me then. They were unmerciful!

We finally took a break for lunch around 11:00 a.m. I was broke down! My back was hurting and I was sticky and itchy all over. I did not want to go back out in the field. I had had enough! I think my grandmother had seen it in my eyes and body language that I was not going to make it through the afternoon. She put me in the barn with the girls lifting and hanging the tobacco. That involved taking the tobacco from the cart, binding the leaves together with string and placing them on a stick about four feet long, and then hanging them in the rafters to dry. That was great for me!

After we left the field and got home, all I wanted to do was to take a bath and go to bed! My second thought was, after working in that tobacco field, I no longer wanted to smoke cigarettes. I did not want to see my girlfriend that night either. I just wanted to catch the next bus back to Baltimore. Picking tobacco was not for me!

That was the hardest work I ever did and I never complained about working hard again on any job. I caught the bus back to Baltimore. I went back to work as a volunteer for Operation Champ. I worked hard teaching gymnastics and I would have happily taken another office job and I have never complained about hard work again!

When I was 17, my girlfriend's father got me a job at Fort McHenry Lumber Company. Getting that job was a great change in my life. I was earning a grown man's wages at seventeen years old.

I started out working from 3:30 p.m. to midnight—the night shift. On the night shift, we also got night differential pay, which took my salary way up. We were able to overlap with the day shift guys and continue production and sometimes got a little overtime.

I got a chance to work around men from all places and stages of life. Some of them had served prison terms and some were still in prison living in half-way houses. There were big men and frail men. Saints and sinners; quiet ones and cursers. Singers, storytellers, and poets.

There were social drinkers, casual drinkers, drunks, alcoholics, and very few non-drinkers. They all worked hard and respected each other. When someone did get out of line or was disrespectful, it was handled right then on the spot. I watched, I listened, and I learned!

Adult Work-life

Following my release of active duty from the Marine Corps, I was supposed to report to play semi-professional football with the Baltimore Eagles, but I found out that the team had folded. So, as a result, I went back to work at Fort McHenry Lumber Company.

Luckily, because I was a dues-paying member of the union, they were obligated to take me back once I fulfilled my military obligations. The lumber company followed the union rules and allowed me to work for 30 days before they laid me off. This enabled me to draw unemployment.

Well, I decided that this was a good time to take a break and enjoy life a little. I was drawing unemployment each week and I had a little money from the leave I turned in and a couple of months' pay from the Corps.

I was also getting money to go to school from the G.I. Bill along with checks each month from the Reserves, so I was okay. At least I thought so. I soon found out that trying to party every night and impress the ladies, help Momma with the rent, keep my car note paid, and everything else to keep it running meant my little nest egg did not last too long.

I knew I needed to find a real job and I did. The Unemployment Office called me one day and told me they had found me a job at General Electric working on the assembly line. It just so happened that my Aunt Irene also worked there, so it was an easy transition.

I started on the day shift working from 7:00 a.m.-3:30 p.m. with the weekends off. We got paid every Monday. I guess that was to make sure everybody came to work that Monday after the weekend. Sweet! I was able to still go to college in the evenings and have time to party with the ladies. Some Friday evenings after work I would hit the road and go straight to North Carolina for the weekend.

Well, that lasted about six months and then we shut down in the summer for two weeks for inventory. When we came back off of the shutdown, some people got moved around and, guess what? I was one of them. I had less seniority so I had to go. I appealed to the Human Resources Department and she welcomed me to the real world of working.

I explained to the Director that when I took the job, I told them I was going to college in the evening and they said that was great! They were all for their employee bettering themselves by going to college. I thought I had gotten thru to her soft heart, but boy was I wrong! She said, "Mr. Cash, you have a choice. You can work here on the evening shift or you can go to college in the evening." Boy, I was not expecting that!

So, yeah, you guessed it. I decided to keep working the evening shift and making the *good* money. But I also starting thinking and was able to get my classes switched to mornings. I learned to make the proper adjustments to everything I was doing before just giving up. Here again, "**I Almost Made IT!**"

General Electric lasted for about a year, and then there was another layoff. I didn't wait around to be called back. On a tip, I landed a job working for the General Services Office of the United States Government as a Federal Protective Officer.

I went down to the Federal Building in Baltimore to apply and, within a couple of months, I was hired. I started as a GS-4 making about $386 every two weeks before taxes. I thought they had to be making some kind of mistake. I was making more than that every week at General Electric!

But it turned out to be good for me. There was a lot of overtime to be made, the work was not so demanding, and I was sent to The Federal Law Enforcement Academy in Glynco, Georgia for training. Even though the instructors were tough and demanding, this place was Disneyland compared to Parris Island. I graduated in the top three of my class of twenty.

As a Federal Protective Officer (FPO), we had three shifts: the day shift from 06:00-14:30; the evening shift from 14:00-2230; and the night shift from 2200-0630.

Again, I started out working the day shift. It was nice to get off early, but it meant being at work by at least 05:30 to draw your weapons, get a briefing, and relieve the midnight shift at least 15 minutes ahead of time so they could leave on time. We had rotating stationary posts, mobile units, and the Panel Room post.

Working a Stationary Post was important. You had to always stay alert and make sure everyone that came through had the proper security badge. I used to try and remember the last names on their badges matching them with their faces. You could learn a lot about people as you moved from post to post. You could also develop a great rapport with the workforce.

Once I had an employee come into the building and come to me in private and inform me that someone had left a briefcase on the bus. We take items like packages and briefcases left unattended very seriously. The thing that made this package more important was that the employee brought it to me from the bus. The employee was new and thought he was doing us a favor by bringing it to me at the Key Desk.

I decided to get one of our other security officers involved also. He always thought that he was better and more skilled than us, so I was going to allow him to show his stuff. I took the briefcase into his office and said, "Look what an employee just gave me." His eyes lit up and you could see the fear on his face. Then I told him to come with me.

My hands were steady and I was confident, so I took the case to a drainage ditch and placed it there, securing the area with sandbags until the EOD Unit arrived and blew it up. Well, to say the least, I was not one of that security officers' favorite people from that day forth.

Afterward, I was given a post away from where he worked and a lot of outside work mostly directing traffic. I guess being a little rebellious did not help my chances of getting a better post.

After a few months, I began to question the fairness of the assignments. Most of us black officers were getting the worst posts, while the white officers were getting to work the Panel Room. In the Panel Room, they had eyes on you and could talk to you. They had coffee and donuts to eat and it was warm in the winter and cool in the summer.

Well, I finally took the advice of a more knowledgeable and wiser officer and confronted my supervisor with my concerns about the unfairness of the assignments. He told me that he could assign me to any post that he wanted to because they were all in my job description. He also informed me that he could not deny me training. He pointed to some books in his office and told me that the answers were there. All I had to do was open the books. Well, I did just that.

After a few months of reading, I took the Corporal Exam and passed it. I was accepted into the second newly formed Special Operations Response Team and was assigned to a mobile unit.

I once again attended the Federal Law Enforcement Academy in Glynco and to Ft. Steward Army Base in Georgia for training. The only thing that I regretted was being moved from the closest place I was working to the more distant Headquarters, but that often comes with a promotion.

Being assigned to a mobile unit was like a senior position. It required that each FPO pass the driver's course and hold a valid driver's license. You also had to be up on local, state, and federal traffic laws and regulations. You also needed to be able to work with other local, state, and federal law enforcement agencies.

After being promoted to Corporal, I was reassigned to Headquarters and given a mobile unit. That is what I did until I graduated from the Federal Law Enforcement Academy's Special Weapons and Tactics Training School.

Then, there was working the Panel Room. Working there, you were considered one of the elite groups by the normal FPO. Most of our senior officers and supervisors came from there. They were the voices over the radios and loudspeakers. This is where all the major decisions were made to keep everyone out of trouble and conflict with federal and state laws and regulations. It took a special temperament to work in the Panel Room and I always tried to avoid that area.

But when I was promoted to Corporal, I not only headed up a squad of the Special Operations Response Team, my place of assignment was the Panel Room. We each were assigned to work in a specific area of the panel. I was very energetic and had a hard time just working in a specific section. I would be moving from one station to another, which caused me to go into another officer's zone. I was driving them crazy. Finally, they could not take it any longer.

They gave me a radio and made me a roving on-call unit. One quiet morning during one of my tours, I was approached by an employee about a suspicious package in a car in the parking lot. That quiet day suddenly became interesting. All of our training was now being used. We secured the area; the EOD Unit was called and the package was removed. All was secured and quiet once again.

Then I was promoted to sergeant. The only downside to being a sergeant was you had to rotate shifts every three months. I had no problem with the day and evening shift, it was that night shift that I could never really get adjusted to.

The officers had developed a code to let everyone know when the supervisors were out making rounds so they could be at their best when they arrived. I had a problem staying awake all night. I knew that some of my officers had the same problem, so when they worked in isolated locations, I would make sure there were three of them there. I would tell them: "It is three of you here. When I come through, somebody better be woke!"

When those posts were inside locked buildings, I would remind the officers that "there should be no way I would catch anyone sleeping, especially when you have to unlock the door to let me in." This worked great most of the time but then you had those that wanted to try you. It did not go well for them. I was a Federal Protective Officer for a little over five years.

EMPLOYMENT/ PROFESSIONAL CAREER

- **File Clerk**

- **Recreation Aide**

- **U.S. Marine Corps**

- **Saw Operator, Ft. McHenry Lumber Co.**

- **Assembler, General Electric**

- **DOD Federal Protective Officer**

- **Private Investigator**

- **Master Plumber/Gas Fitter**

- **DOD Facilities Manager**

- **DOD Project Manager**

- **DOD Property Officer**

- **Logistics Officer**

- **Training Consultant**

- **Karate/Boxing/Kickboxing Instructor**

Choices We Make in Life

One of my big turnarounds came in my job as a Federal Protective Officer. The 70s was a time of racial unrest in our nation, as we still see today. As young black men, we were always trying to prove ourselves to be as good as the other races, mainly the whites. This happened especially, as it is quietly kept, in government workplaces.

Once you got that government job, you thought the struggle was over. Wrong! Racism was more deliberate there than anywhere else. We would try to stand firm in our "blackness" and challenge the system in our own way. Some of us would take the menial jobs to avoid not becoming known as a yes man or labeled "an Uncle Tom."

Some of the officers I worked with would be threatened to be fired and/or had retired from the Baltimore City Police Department because they were involved in racial incidents. Some of us were fresh off of active duty in the military and others were just getting out of college.

I always tried to stay out of the way of the racial conversations and rebelled in my own way. I decided that I would do just enough to keep the supervisor off my back. I was a "minute man" and used all my annual and sick leave as fast as I got it. As soon as I got off the post, I would find somewhere to go to sleep and dare the supervisors to say anything to me.

One day, I was working a traffic post and there was a loudspeaker on that post. I could hear the other officers in the Panel Room laughing and enjoying themselves. It was cold and raining and I started thinking, "I am really showing them who the man is! They are sitting in that nice warm Panel Room, with hot coffee and doughnuts, with their warm breakfast. I am out here cold, wet, hungry, wanting a hot cup of coffee, but I am really showing them."

So, on one of my breaks, I went and talked to my sergeant. I asked him what could I do to start working in the Panel Room sometimes. He told me that I needed to be dependable and professional. He also told me that he could assign me to any post he wanted, but he could not deny me training. At that time, he pointed to the library of books in his office and told me that anything I needed to know about the job and the regulations were in those books, so I should try reading them. I got the message loud and clear!

I requested training and started coming to work early and began reading those books every chance I got. Not long after that, I was placed in the Panel Room and being assigned to the vehicles. I started seeing another side of law enforcement and liking it. I applied for the Corporal position that came available and got it. I was finally moving.

I was selected for the Special Operation and Response Team and became the team leader. The next year a Sergeant slot became available. I applied and got it.

I had been a Sergeant in the Marine Corps and I knew how to supervise men, so this was right in my domain. I worked well with my officers and looked out for them.

My teams were the best at our site and I could ask them to do anything and it was done with no hassles. Even after I left the force, I was still invited to shoot at the marksmanship competition and I always placed in the top three.

I was also able to attend training that was mainly for law enforcement personnel. So, my decision to be my own man and not settle for the status quo worked out for me and helped me move on in my career.

I also used my five years of law enforcement experience and knowledge while working as a Federal Protective Officer to obtain a Maryland State Private Investigators License under All County Security. While working under their umbrella, I formed my own security/personal protection company on the side. I did security for large chain restaurants like "Chuck E Cheese" and major hardware stores like "Home Depot" as well as private security for politicians, businessmen, and athletes.

Eventually, I was able to earn promotions and make more money with All County Security. And, in my outside businesses, I earned extra money while gaining more knowledge and making more social and business connections. So that one smart choice to go back to school, in the end, allowed me to retire with over 41 years of service and receive a nice pension for my troubles.

One evening I was talking to my friend and trainer Jerry Boorts, and he said to me, "I know you like what you do, but you need to get out of that uniform. You need to get a trade, something you can fall back on."

So while making my rounds in one of the buildings one night, I searched the vacancy announcement board and found a vacancy announcement for plumbing apprentices. When I read it, all the right things for me were in there: 07:00-15:30! Those were the keywords. I did not care what the job was—all I cared about was 07:00-15:30.

Jerry helped me fill out the government application, by suggesting the keywords they wanted to see. When I was selected, everyone wanted to know why I was leaving. It was predicted by my fellow officers that I would make lieutenant within the next year. My answer to them was 07:00-15:30! I transferred over to Facility Support and started my next venture.

There, I attended a four-year plumbing apprenticeship program, once again graduating in the top five of my class. The whole time I was in the program, the plumbers already there kept saying that I would never be a plumber. The foreman kept reminding me that I was not a supervisor anymore. My friend Jerry Boorts, who was my guardian angel, would come to my defense. They did not like Jerry, because he knew his stuff and could outtalk them and he was the Vice President of the Trade Union. Jerry really smacked them in the face by making me the Shop Steward for the

Union. This still did not stop them from giving me the dirty and ditch-digging jobs.

When sewage cables needed to be cleaned and pipes needed to be dug up, even though we had hoses and a backhoe, I had to do it by hand. But I never complained.

They came to respect me and started teaching me. When I started doing jobs on the side, they would make sure I used all the right parts and even sometimes helped me. They would also have me help them with their outside work. In the shop I became the materials' purchaser where I was introduced to the major vendors and suppliers.

With their mentoring and supervision, three years later I became a Master Plumber and Gas Fitter. I started my own plumbing company and named it *Three C's Plumbing and Drain Cleaning*. I named it that in hopes that my sons would join me someday or take it over.

Several years later the government decided to reorganize and all of the individual shops were consolidated into one huge Facility Management Organization. The Union was dissolved and we were all divided into teams and given specific areas of responsibility.

A new concept was introduced: "Doing More with Less." Under this concept, many teams were formed and tasked with coming up with ideas to improve the way we did business. One team was formed that studied the use of manpower and the training of the mechanical workforce.

Jerry was on this team and made the observation that there were no blacks or women on the team. After being victorious with his case to upper management, he suggested that I become a part of this team and he also selected a black female, who worked in the front office.

Our team investigated and researched the distribution of manpower and training. We developed and provided graphs, statistics, and charts to substantiate our findings to upper management. They empowered us to develop a training lab to be used in the cross-training of the existing workforce.

The training included carpenters, electricians, heating ventilation and air conditioning mechanics, and Plumbers/Gas Fitters. The training lab was built by members of the existing workforce and with excess material from renovation projects and donated materials from vendors and suppliers we did business with. It was built in strategic areas of the building so the mechanics remained accessible to their areas of responsibility during training.

Once everything was set up, I was able to convince our team that their idea to have a "Multi-Skilled Workforce" would take years to develop. What they were talking about was to have the mechanics cross-train in carpentry, electrical, HVAC, and plumbing through accredited trade schools. This would take three to four years for each trade.

I convinced them that we needed something that could meet the needs of our stakeholders immediately: a "Multi-Functional Workforce." The mechanics would learn the basics of the trades and be able to isolate the problem until the proper mechanic was available to fix it. This would minimize damage to the facility and inconvenience to the customer.

From that training concept, I was able to develop and have approved an agency-wide, thirteen-week course called "The Multi-Functional Workforce." Our team went on to win the highest award given in that era for training: the "Golden Hammer Award." When we went to receive the award, Jerry had me stand in front with him holding the award. Again, they did not want me to take credit for the training course, but again Jerry thought differently. He told me they had given him a cash award and he shared the award money with me.

Golden Hammer Award 1999 Me and Jerry "Almost Made IT"

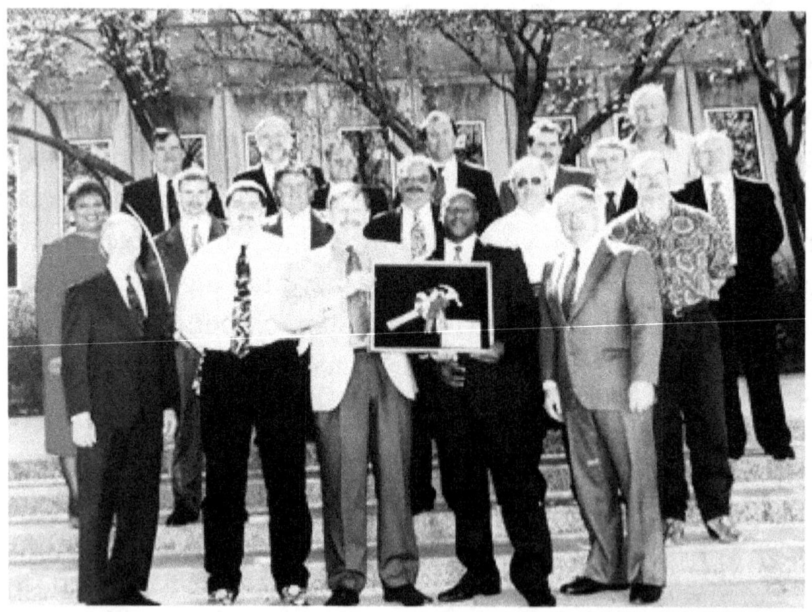

After the team concept faded away, I transferred over to the Project Manager Division. I was the Project Manager for Small Projects. These projects were small renovations, alterations, and repair by replacements costing less than $100K.

I started taking all kinds of self-paced training courses in Project Management, Facility Management, Electrical, Plumbing, HVAC, Construction, and other related courses. I became very knowledgeable and earned numerous certifications in Project Management, Facility Management, and Training. I began traveling up and down the Baltimore-Washington Corridor managing projects.

My name was rapidly getting around the Front Office. I then was asked to become the Organization Training Coordinator. This was a newly created position that came out of one of the other teams' recommendations. The position was kept quiet and not advertised as usual.

I was told just to put my name on a piece of paper, so I did just that. Well, once I took office, they realized that I was only a GS-09 and I was supervising GS-09, 11, and 13s from different branches of the organization. I was immediately promoted to GS-11. I was given my own office, secretary, and authorization to draw vehicles from the Motor Pool.

As the Training Coordinator, I was responsible for overseeing all the training being done in the entire organization. I had access to the entire organization's workforce records. So I had access to all the little secrets, so to say, but I never misused my office privileges and authority.

I had always noticed how unfairly training was allocated and it was my time to fix it. I got the opportunity to attend trade shows, colleges, exposés, etc. In my first year, I was able to help 12 members of the custodial workforce get their GED high school graduation certificates. Most of them were facing the prospect of their jobs being outsourced, but I was also able to get them in training programs that provided them with more marketable skills and some went on to get into college.

I helped others that worked in offices and were in supervision to earn college credits, get accreditations, and maintain accreditations they had earned. I also helped the trades personnel to expand their skills into higher-level sections of their specific trades. Trades personnel were also able to get into training that they needed to perform their jobs daily and to stay current with technology.

As I said earlier, I had always noticed how the training was unfairly provided. The office workforce got most of the better training at the preferred places, while the trades personnel were denied what they needed or sent to the second-rate places. So I started to take a look at who was putting in for what training.

I checked their training records to make sure the right person was going to the appropriate courses. Most of the time, they did not match up and I would deny them that training. I once told the supervisors that I knew what was going on, but I did not mind sending them to the training as long as they took the person that needed the training the most with them.

Once I started scrutinizing the training requests, things started to change for me. My office was taken from me and I was moved into the open work area. I had no more office to talk confidentially with the personnel. I had no more walls to put up posters, training announcements, etc.

The second-year is when it all came to a head. I had just received the training funding for the entire year. I went to a two-week class and, when I came back, I was told that the Division Chiefs had gotten together and decided that they no longer needed a Training Coordinator.

Extremely upset, I went into my Division Chief's office and told her that "you and the other division chiefs make decisions that affect the entire workforce and you do not have a clue as to what the workforce really needs to do their jobs." After that, I was told that my Division Chief wanted me out of her air space, that "she did not care where I went, she wanted me gone." So I was exiled to another facility that few people knew about.

The transfer to the Facility Management Division began my career as a Facility Manager. I managed 13 facilities along the Baltimore-Washington Corridor to the Pentagon in Arlington, Virginia, and the surrounding area. I relieved a friend of mine name Jeff. Jeff was also a good friend of Jerry.

Jeff was a good HVAC mechanic and had been managing this facility for a long time. He was always relaxed in his attire and in running the facility. He went on TDY a lot and got to know a lot of people from other agencies. They wanted him to work full-time with a partner, so they needed someone to take his place and that became me.

I was told by my supervisor that I would only be out there for one month while they were waiting for someone to answer the vacancy announcement and then I would go to a facility closer to Baltimore.

One month went past, then a couple more. By that time I was back in college and realized that I had plenty of time to study as no one was bothering me. I only went to the office when we had meetings on Friday. I just had to call in when I got to work in the morning and when I left in the evening.

It was nice—trees, fresh air, no one looking over my shoulder, and the Chief of Station and tenants liked me. I was the man! I called my supervisor one day and told him I preferred to stay out there and they should keep the new person with them.

I spent the next three years out there by myself. I was on-call 24 hours but it was okay. Everything ran smoothly and I very rarely ran into problems. I started being asked to go TDY to other countries, the first being Germany. I got there on the 9th of September, the Sunday before 9/11. Suddenly, our whole mission changed!

I was transferred from being a plumber back to an armed security officer. This lasted a couple of days and then I was back on the original job. We ended up getting extended because of being shut down by the threat. We were behind schedule and our relief team was not coming out.

Little did we know that as a result of the attack on the U.S., our freedom of movement had been redirected and minimized. When we got back to the U.S., we found that our safe and peaceful world had changed. There were barricades and security forces everywhere. I had security projects waiting for me at each of my facilities. To manage all the additional projects, we had additional staff assigned to our team. I was not going to be alone anymore; I now had a partner.

My new partner knew very little about Project Management and nothing about Facility Management. So, now, my training hat was back on and I was able to get him into training classes to help him learn our business.

After two years, he informed me that he was trying to get promoted and needed to be in the spotlight where he could be seen. I advised and helped him get a job at the main campus. He was successful in getting recognized and getting promoted.

Then they sent me another partner, Ed. I had known Ed back at General Electric. He was a very cool, down-to-earth brother. I had run into him again on the security force and then in the apprenticeship program. He was an electrician by trade and he was good at it.

He was easy to talk to and he was a Mason. He traveled a lot TDY as an electrician and understood project management and a little of facility management. We had a lot in common and this matchup worked, so we had each other's back. He was planning on retiring within the next two years and because he was very outspoken, he needed to be somewhere out of the management's sight.

When I went TDY, Ed held down the fort. My last time out was in Iraq, Afghanistan, and Qatar. I was at a briefing and saw my friend Jim on the screen. He was in his late 60s and had surgery before he left. He had been out there for over a year with no relief and he looked very tired.

After seeing that, I volunteered to go to Qatar to help him. In preparation for my TDY, I had training in shooting and servicing weapons, high-speed pursuit, defensive and offensive driving, surveillance and counter-surveillance, Arabic language and customs, and the issuing and collection of uniforms and equipment.

We were a forward logistics team that received and escorted personnel, equipment, and material in transit to U.S. Air Force bases in Iraq and Afghanistan. There we set up and scheduled transportation, lodging, and storage for the warfighters. At times, we also received and escorted classified equipment and materials to their destinations.

It was a two-man operation. We lived in a small one-or two-man room on the base and we worked out of a large tent that also served as a warehouse, communications center, and armory. We always kept our phones on because you never knew when you might get a phone call with someone on the other end in trouble or needing to get escorted from the airport in Doha to the base. We worked 16-18 hours each day easily. I would sleep with my phone right by my ear.

We would usually get a message about who or what was coming and when and have time to schedule it. But other times as soon as you lay down your phone, it would ring and you would have to go. They gave you a ration card to buy beer—nothing stronger was available—but during the four months I was there, I never used it. You always had to be ready to go and you did not know what you were going to encounter outside of the base.

Two of our vehicles had been blown up before I arrived. The locals were very rich. They bought a license first and then a car. It was nothing to see cars turned over on the roads, mostly straight roads.

I learned that respect goes a long way. My predecessor told me how he would get shot at when going to and from the airport. I realized that his fear made him disrespect the local people so that when they saw an American, they would try to kill them. Some of the safety procedures he taught me I just threw out the window. I relied on common sense and respect, and with caution, I had no real problems.

My tour there was really good and I did not want to leave, but my other commitments and my upcoming divorce hearing made it essential that I come back at that time. I had one week to train my replacement. I thought it would be a piece of cake. I read his resume and he had attended more prestigious combat training schools than any of us had. We thought we had a "super" agent coming.

After the first drive to Doha Airport, we knew that what was written was not the real person we had. We all were cautious and took the job and reality of getting killed or captured very seriously, but we were willing to put our lives and safety aside for our customers. He was reluctant to go to the airport and when he got there, he refused to get out of the vehicle and go inside. He kept saying, "What if they blow up the vehicle?" I kept telling him, "What if they blow it up with you in it?"

One of the major parts of our job was to go into the airport and escort the client to the vehicle and then to the Air Force Base safely. You had to go inside and get the client. While you were inside, you were under surveillance by their agents. After a while, you recognized them and they recognized you. You would respectfully smile at one another and continue with your business. I never had an incident with them.

Well, my replacement did not complete the tour. A couple of weeks after I returned to the U.S., they asked me to go back out there to relieve him until they could get someone else. I did have an incident with one of our Marine clients coming through Customs. I was not allowed to go beyond the baggage counter at the airport, but you could see the people coming out and those going through inspection. That night, I saw my client being inspected and talking to the inspector.

I said to myself, "Please be quiet. Please be quiet!" I thought the fact that he was a U.S. Marine Captain meant that he knew to be quiet. Well, all of a sudden, I saw them with some rifle magazines in their hand, and then after he said something else, I saw them dump his suitcases and throw his items everywhere. Finally, everything settled down and they let him go through, however, they kept the magazines.

He came out complaining that they kept his magazines and the only thought in my mind was, "Why would you bring your personal magazines to the Middle East anyway?" He complained all the way back to the base and I had to tell him to let us handle anything that might happen.

As soon as I got him squared away, I sent a message back telling them what happened and requesting that they tell everyone traveling to us to keep their mouths shut when coming through airport security. We cannot do anything for them while they are in their custody. And please do not bring ammo, weapons, or any other weapons-related items with you.

By the time I left, he still had not gotten those magazines back. What I did at that site was so important to the United States Global War on Terrorism efforts that I received the Secretary of Defense Medal.

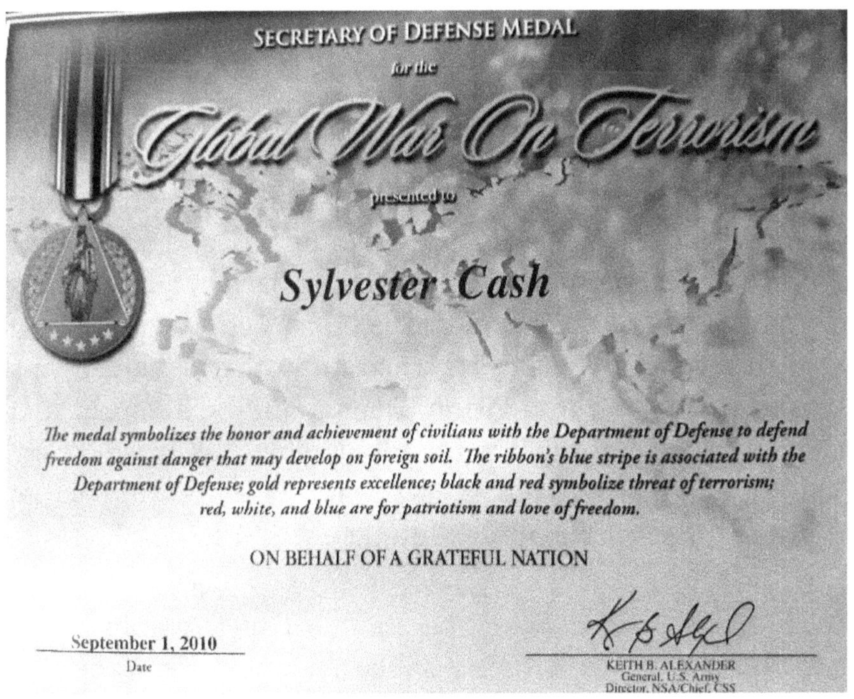

Before I left there, a message came out that promotion packets had to be submitted before a certain date and the Team Leader position was coming available. All of the paperwork had to be in by a date that I would not be able to meet because of where I was at the time. My Team Leader told me to let him know if I was interested and he would put my name forward. So that is what I did.

I tried to put my promotion package in, but because of the systems we had, I was unable to access the information that I needed. So as soon as I hit the states, before going home, I went to the office and submitted my promotion package. A couple of days later, I received a message informing me that my packet was returned because it was late and I received a message telling me that the Team Leader position had been filled by someone from outside of the organization. My other co-workers told me that they said in an open meeting that they knew I would be upset. A double whammy!

My first step was to approach them about my promotion packet. I went up the chain of command and they were ordered to accept my packet. I turned it back in and the next day I received it back as unqualified. I was good with that; at least they accepted it and returned it. So then I requested a face-to-face with our Division Chief about the Team Leader position, I had known him for a long while and trusted him. The last thing he said to me was, "They owe you an explanation and I will make sure they give it to you."

Well, I got to meet with the Branch Chief, whom I had known for a very long time just like everyone else. I knew he was a part of the "good ole boy group." We talked and he explained to me "that I did not have enough exposure in the Facility Management arena and nobody knew me."

I explained to him that I had been a Facility Manager for eight years and was the senior manager on the team. Also, I was the Training Coordinator before and got training for all of them and they exiled me because I knew they were misusing the training funds, so "how did they not know me?"

Then he went on to talk about education. When he said to me, "You need more education for this position," I asked, "How much education do I need? I only have a Master's Degree. Is that not enough?" Again I asked, "What is the criteria for the Team Leader Position so I can prepare myself if it comes up again?" He then went quiet and asked me to leave. I never got an answer so I filed an EEO Complaint. They came back and said I had not filed it within the proper time limits.

That evening while I was in the market buying groceries, I received a phone call asking me to go to Afghanistan. After making sure the call was legitimate, I told them to call me at work on the secure line to discuss it. Ed said, "Cash they just finished telling you that you are useless this whole week. You filed an EEO Complaint on them and now they need you to go back over there. Man, they are trying to kill you. You are not supposed to come back. Watch your back!"

With one-day notice, I was taken to Dover Air Force Base and put on a plane to Germany with two large crates, no orders, and no itinerary. I arrived in Germany and was met and escorted to a hanger with the crates. The Airmen knew my sister, Pam, so they found me a place to sleep with the crates in a guarded area and brought me food for a day and a half until the next flight left.

I arrived in Bagram, Afghanistan, and was relieved of the crates. During that time, they were removing mines from the fields around the runway. I saw dogs and small children running up and down the area they were sweeping. I cringed each time I saw one running through there.

I still had no orders but I had my Department of Defense Identification. With that, I was able to contact my old team at Al-Udeid Air Base and have them schedule me a flight there and then to the U.S. I met a group of soldiers that had been trying for a week to get a flight out. I told them to get a flight to Al-Udeid Air Base and they could move out from there, but they did not listen to me and they were still there when I left.

It was there that I learned to appreciate the USO and all they do. I spent two days there and they made me as comfortable as they could. I never appreciated coffee and popcorn so much.

I flew to Al-Udeid Air Base and then back to Dover within a week. They were shocked to see that I had returned so quickly. They had forgotten that I had helped others move around in the theater so I knew what worked, plus I had friends out there.

Well, once I got settled back in, the fight for justice was on. I met with the Assistant Division Chief whom I had helped get a lot of training and accreditations when I was the

Training Coordinator and who also was a Masonic Brother. He told me that with my background I should be nothing less than a Branch Chief. He even divulged to me that he didn't have the master's degree they were telling me I needed. He then pulled out the organizational chart and showed me that there was nothing available as a Branch Chief, but, after I left for overseas, twelve Branch Chief positions were created.

He then advised me to consider getting into a smaller pond. He contacted a couple of others and had me meet with them. They talked to me about PCSing to Japan as the Station Facility Manager. I had been approached about Korea years before but the time was not right for me and I declined. But this time, they came to me differently. They talked about overseas pay, the increase in retirement points, benefits, etc. It sounded good to me and the timing was right. Kenneth had completed high school and my divorce was final. There was nothing to keep me there.

Then they came back with Korea on the table again. It seemed that something happened with the person that was supposed to go to Korea—that he could not go there and they needed to send him to Japan instead. Well, the presentation was still good and I was getting more money than going to Japan and a different job title. I agreed. I started taking Korean language classes and I was off to Seoul, Korea as a Program Manager for three years.

I arrived in Seoul in September 2007 and the weather was starting to change but it was still not cold yet. It was the same as the weather in Baltimore so I was okay. I hit the ground running.

Negotiations were going on for the relocation of our facility. I was in awe of those around the table: The Korean delegation, U.S. generals, colonels, politicians, and then little ole me, GS-12. I felt like this was way over my head, so I got back into the books and re-familiarized myself with the language. The main thing that was saving me was that I did not have to say anything because there were others there that had been in this fight for a while. And no one wanted to sit next to me!

After a couple of months there, I was told that I was under the Facility Management Division. This was disturbing to me. I was under the impression that I was finally moving up in the organization as a staff member, now to find out that I was still a Facility Manager known to them as the Facility's guy! Being a Facilities guy is not a bad or degrading thing, it is just that I thought I was finally getting a place at the table.

I remember at one of the negotiation meetings everyone was coming in and taking seats at the table, but I thought it was best to take a seat along the wall. Some of the others kept telling me to move to the table, but I declined. I was comfortable where I was.

As all the higher ranks came into the room, some of those sitting at the table were asked to leave the table so other officers could sit there. Those were the same ones that had tried to get me to sit at the table. You could see it on their faces; they were feeling pretty embarrassed and degraded. You could hear a pin drop in the room. The almighty ones had just been dethroned.

One of the others came to me and asked me why I never sit at the table and I told him that I learned from the Bible that "you should wait to be asked to sit at the table, before assuming you are the privileged one." After a year, the negotiations were still at a standstill. The only thing that we did get funded was our motor pool. I think the only reason for that was because it was standard and without any extra features. Also, that was one of the few times that I said something. What I said was: "The longer we keep trying to nickel and dime this project the more expensive it is going to be. Things are constantly going up and so is the price of this project."

I returned to the U.S. to attend a Facility roundtable; it was quite interesting. While there, I overheard a conversation that my boss and his longtime friend/former boss were having. The former boss expressed his desire to return to work back in Korea.

When we got back to Korea, my Boss called me to the side and asked me would I consider moving from the Program Manager position to the Facility Manager position after the Facility Manager retired. He went on to explain the benefits of doing that and that he would also support my promotion to GS-14. Well, to me that was the selling point!

I took over that position and was promoted soon afterward. I did such a good job that they asked me to stay on as the Station Chief, who would retire in a couple of years. But I had already negotiated and been offered a position as Chief of Installations and Logistics in Thailand. So my reply to them was, "Why should I wait for the Chief here to retire when I can get my own station now? Also, I am older than him."

So after Korea, I moved on to Thailand and finished up my forty-plus-year career as the Chief of Installation and Logistics in Thailand. After the United States, the TDYs, and South Korea, Thailand was like the retirement place. Even when I interviewed for the job, it was a relaxed atmosphere, much different from most places I had worked. The Chief of Station told me I would be working from 07:00-15:30 like clockwork. He told me there would be a driver to pick me up for work each morning and bring me home in the evening. When I asked about overtime, he said there would be none. "NONE?" I thought to myself while thinking he really did not know what my job entailed as the Chief of Installations and Logistics. So, I asked, "What if the chillers go down at night and the systems start overheating? Or what if a water line breaks after hours and the facility floods?"

He enlightened me that no one would be calling me in and it would not be my responsibility to respond to it. If something were to happen, it would be something that I would take care of the next day. He also informed me that he knew of my reputation of being a hard worker, but whatever I did not finish that day could wait until the next day. I was still thinking to myself, "This cannot be real. He is just joking with me!"

Well, at the end of my interview, he asked me one question and said: "Be careful how you answer it. Your employment might depend on it." The question was, "Do you play golf?" My answer was, "I don't know how to play but I am willing to learn." He said, "Welcome aboard!"

In my previous job locations, we had a staff of personnel to take care of administrative, logistical, and operational aspects of Installation and Logistics. To put it softly, there I had a staff of five and we handled everything from facility management, project management, and logistics to communications, transportation, etc. My Thai counterpart was as hard of a worker as I was and, after I taught him a few other skills, he was awesome. I'm sure that is why I was so successful.

When my co-workers were off playing golf and relaxing, my team and I were hard at work getting things done that were hard to do when they worked within the facilities. I would schedule only to get the essential things completed so my team could relax with the rest of the workforce. I would even get the opportunity to set-up the grill and barbeque for our host and they began to look forward to it. Even though a three-year tour of duty turned into a five-year tour, I still maintained the same work ethics as I came in with and was known by all to be the hardest and most dependable worker there. But I never learned to play golf.

After about ten years or more in the Facilities arena, things continued to be unfair to us in promotions, awards, and training. After returning from a deployment to the desert, I finally had enough and decided to confront the Front Office. It started with my decision to put my name in the hat for the position of Team Leader that was coming available. I knew that there was no one on the east coast better at Facility Management than me.

I had managed ten facilities single-handedly for over eight years. I had taken all of the necessary formal classes and training in Facility Management. I had more than a basic understanding of facility mechanical, plumbing, and electrical systems and construction. Coming from security, I knew the security policies and protocol. Taking all of these qualifications into consideration, I felt that I should have been a shoo-in for that position. It was a "no brainer!"

It did not happen as I thought it would. They brought in from another organization a person who knew nothing about facilities, much less Facility Management. On my transit back from my tour in the Middle East, I was told of their selection. I was not happy about that decision and talk was already coming from our Branch Manager about it. I knew it was blatant disrespect and a blatantly unfair personnel decision.

So my question to them was simply, "What was the criteria for the position?" A very simple question to me! They would never answer that question. After meeting with management at various levels, one of them told me that I should "consider getting in a smaller pond and taking an overseas tour." I decided to consider the advice given and in the upcoming weeks, I researched the vacancy announcements for overseas positions. I had places in mind where I wanted to go, but they wanted me to go to Japan.

I was accepted as the Installations and Logistics Chief in Japan. But as soon as that decision was made, I was asked not to accept that position but to take a position in Seoul, Korea as Program Manager for the relocation of the facility. I had been asked to go to Korea about five or six years earlier, but the time was not right to leave. I was in my master's degree program, writing my thesis, and, more importantly, Kenneth was in high school and I did not want to leave him during that phase of his life. By not taking that position at that time, for several years I was systematically "blackballed" for any overseas assignment.

However, the next time was right. I was finished with school, all my children were done with high school, and I had just completed my divorce so there was nothing left to keep me from going. I learned early in life that with every choice we make, there are costs associated with it. In that case, the costs were numerous and far greater than I had imagined.

First, I had to relocate to an entirely different world and culture. That meant closing up my house, shutting down my plumbing and security businesses, and my karate and kickboxing schools. Next, I had to give up my positions as a Trustee and Financial Secretary at my church. Finally, and more importantly, I was not going to be there physically to help my grandsons grow and mature.

I got the opportunity to learn and be a part of the political side of negotiations in Project Management. This led to an increase in my professional contacts. The next year, I was asked to take over the Facility Management position, which led to more money because overtime was necessary. That promotion increased my salary and retirement benefits.

Before I started into the retirement stage, and even when I entered that stage of my life, I made some major choices and decisions. One of, if not the most profound major decisions of my life, was when I made God number one. It not only changed my life, but it helps me every day to cope with the trials and tribulations of life. I've learned to put my faith in God.

When I was a small child, my momma would send us to church. As I got older, when I would get into trouble, she would make me go to church as punishment. I am probably just like so many of the rest of you; I never knew how important church would become in my life. I have tried several times to read the entire Bible, but I do not ever remember completing it. When the time comes to seek the Lord's guidance, somehow, I am guided to the right passage in the Holy Scripture.

After I had been competing for several years in karate tournaments and on the kickboxing circuits, I found myself feeling kind of empty. I was making good money, had plenty of women, opened a karate school and kickboxing academy, was world ranked, and I had all that I was trying to get. It seemed like I was supposed to feel like I was on top of the world yet I didn't!

After training one day with my good friend and karate schoolmate Steve, we started talking. I explained to him how I was feeling empty inside and it had nothing to do with women. He asked me to come to church with him on Sunday and I agreed. Then I started thinking to myself, church?

That Sunday I met him at Providence Baptist Church. I felt so peaceful and fulfilled at that service. I began to go to the 07:45 a.m. service every Sunday.

I started out sitting in the back of the church and, one day, I felt that I needed to get closer to the front and closer to

Christ. I moved closer and sat on the fifth pew in the middle aisle every Sunday. On my birthday I decided to give my life to Christ as my birthday present to myself. I was fortunate that my momma was there to witness my baptism.

As time went on, I became a member of the Inspirational Singers Choir. Being shy, I always stayed in the background singing. Whenever they asked that I sing a solo, I would tell them that I liked making my "joyful noise" in the back.

One Sunday I was talking to the President of the Usher Board, Brother Cunningham, and he told me that I needed to be standing at the gates with him. It just happened I had been thinking the same thing, so I joined the Usher Board and faithfully manned the doors each Sunday. I felt a sense of pride and pleasure welcoming members and visitors to our church each Sunday.

I assisted the Trustees in keeping the church clean and doing small plumbing jobs that needed to be done. I offered my professional facility management, project management, and plumbing knowledge and expertise when services were contracted out. Afterward, I was elected to the Trustee Board and appointed as the Church Financial Secretary.

Each Sunday I was there to open the church with the Deacon. I tried to be the first one there, but for some reason, I could never get there before the Deacon. I would also be the last one to leave the church each Sunday evening with the Treasurer to deposit the church collections in the bank.

My decision to give my life to Christ has not only enabled me to become more spiritual but also more compassionate.

I gave a lot of my professional services for little or no cost to those that could not afford plumbing services.

 I also provided physical security services to the church for free and security equipment installation at cost. I would read scriptures on Sundays and other occasions when needed. I went to visit the sick at hospitals and their homes.

I was once asked to pray one Sunday and I responded that I was not a Deacon. I was told as a church trustee I was like a Deacon and needed to know scripture and be able to pray. So, from that point on, I was always willing to pray. In fact, I really love to pray.

A big change came in my life while serving in an overseas location while providing services for the "War on Terrorism". Being in the Marine Corps, I still had that Marine mentality: kill, kill, kill! Most units that I served with were military and because of my appearance and fitness, along with my GS-14 grade which is equivalent to a Lieutenant Colonel, they thought that I was still in the Marine Corps.

One day, while watching the monitor in the Operations Center, something came over me. We were monitoring an operation of our troops. During the final phase, I witnessed people dying like in the movies, but this was not a movie, it was real. I think God touched my heart and, for the first time, I got emotional about it. Don't get me wrong, I am for our troops doing the jobs they are doing, but I no longer applaud seeing people die, especially the innocent. Since then, I have been very sentimental about violent deaths and families of the victims. I continue to pray for world peace and families of the victims of unnecessary violence.

Even before I planned to retire, I decided that Thailand would be a great place to live. I like the weather, the accessibility to other countries, the pretty women, and the food. As I tell all that ask why I don't want to go back to the States, my answer to them is, "I don't ever want to be cold again!"

I Made It!

Chapter 7

Retirement

Retirement Day: October 2, 2015

Khun Patrawadee, Debbie, Sunee, Cash and Somphong

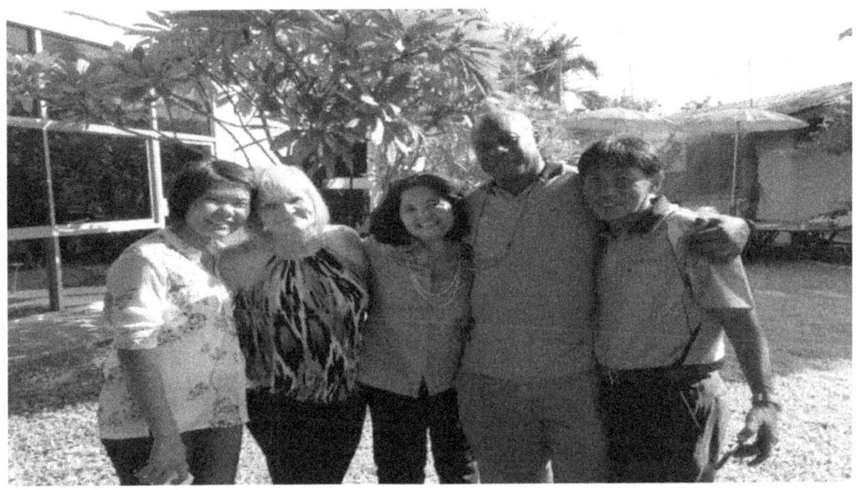

I always liked cooking and when I was in the Marine Corps, I even contemplated opening up a restaurant once I got out. But somehow this career always avoided me.

In Boot Camp, we had what they call a "Mess and Maintenance Week" after finishing the Rifle Range and going into your 3rd Phase of training. You were assigned to work in the Mess Hall or do maintenance work on the grounds of the buildings on Parris Island during the day and pull Guard Duty at night. Well, I was never selected to work in the Mess Hall, always on Guard Duty.

After graduating from Boot Camp, I was assigned to the 2nd Shore Party Battalion, 2nd Marine Division, Camp Lejeune, North Carolina. While waiting to go to communications school we were assigned to do two weeks of Mess Duty or two weeks of Guard Duty. Yes, you guessed it, I again drew the Guard Duty. For some reason, I would never get assigned to Mess Duty. Maybe it was because they somehow knew that I would be comfortable there.

When we went out into the field, we ate what they called at that time "Sea Rats." These meals were emergency meals and had been sitting in storage since who knows when. They consisted of a wide variety of meals: ham & eggs, spaghetti, pork slices, beef and potatoes, tuna, and beans & franks.

They also had treats in them like peaches, pound cake, chewing gum, chocolates, and cigarettes. In the beginning, you did not know what you would get, but the more you were in the field, the wiser you became when selecting "Sea Rats." They were nothing like the modern-day MREs; they were gourmet meals! So, I always carried hot sauce or tabasco sauce, onions, salt, and pepper in my pack.

We had steel helmets so I would take the steel pot out and use it to cook and spice these meals up. We would trade off meals and combine meals to develop a gourmet meal, or at least we considered it to be. I would also pull snails off the rocks, catch small crabs from the shores of the beaches where we landed.

Sometimes we were there for weeks. We would catch bugs and find wild onions to add to our bland meals. All these gourmet delights were added to the pot and the outcome was different every time, but it made our meals more challenging and, most of the time, pleasing.

I used to dream about having my own rib and chicken shack. There was a place on Baker Street and Fulton Avenue in Baltimore. They had the best chicken and pork ribs that you ever wanted to taste. When we lived on that side of town, that was the Friday or Saturday night treat. If not there, it was Sampson's near downtown. Their dinners also "were off the hook!"

Upon coming back home to Baltimore, I did not think about cooking as much. I wanted to play football and just get a job. The only time I thought about cooking was when we had family reunions or one of the families had a cookout. During those events, my Uncle Charles and Uncle Sidney usually did the cooking and grilling. My momma and my Aunts took care of the potato salad, greens, cornbread, fried chicken, pork dishes, cakes, pies, and of course, banana pudding.

For years I waited and waited to get my chance to show off my stuff on the grill. Finally, when I was 40 years old, I got up the nerve and asked the question, "How old do I have to be to cook on the grill?" You could hear a pin drop, but it was not until then that my uncles started to show me things on the grill. They did not let me take over, but they showed me things. It was not until they passed away that I started grilling regularly for the family functions.

In the beginning, I burned a few test pieces of chicken and maybe ribs. But they were test pieces! After then, my sisters and female cousins started saying I burn everything. "Keep him off the grill!" I did not, and still don't, pay them any mind. We all just laughed.

I would be on the grill from three to four hours before things started and stayed until the very end. The grill was and still is my comfort zone.

Between those times, I loved to entertain my friends by grilling and cooking. I had a grill that sat on my back porch year-round so I could grill at any time. I especially enjoyed cooking for ladies. I had a very small apartment and I used to set my living room up like a restaurant dining room using fold-up chairs and a table. I called it "Cash's Place." I had adjustable dimming lights, drinks, soft music, soft pillows, and a carpeted floor.

Becoming an activity member in the Masonic Order gave me another opportunity to learn about preparation, cooking, and hospitality. I met Brothers that had these techniques down to a science. I learned about knowing your customers, understanding relationships, who best can work together, and who could talk the talk, along with who could get things done.

I was taught about meats and different temperatures. One of my biggest lessons was "if you need a knife to cut ribs apart, then you should not eat those ribs." Each year, we would prepare meals and refreshments for over 1,000 Brothers. These Brothers, their companions, and friends traveled from as far as Connecticut in the Northeast and South Carolina in the Southeast for a weekend of fellowship in Baltimore, Maryland. No one ever left dissatisfied or hungry.

Service-orientated events are an art within themselves. Servicing the public is a whole different animal and takes special people with special skills and training. I watched these Brothers do it and take it to another level. I have watched others cook for years. I have watched cooking shows and I have dabbled in cooking.

After a year or so of retirement, I start thinking about things that I wanted to do all my life but had not done. The first thing was traveling to other countries and the next was cooking. So I decided to incorporate the two. In every country that I visited, I included a one-day cooking class on my itinerary. (I still do.) I have attended classes in Bangkok, Saigon, Bali, and Phnom Phen.

I started thinking about things I really wanted to do all these years and what popped into my mind was taking a cooking class. I wanted to take a formal class and experience formal training.

I have no desire to be a chef, open a restaurant, or be a manager of a cooking establishment. I just wanted to learn something I have always been curious about. I wanted to be able to understand what they were talking about on TV. I wanted to be able to prepare edible meals for my friends.

While in these classes, I was reminded of my good friend and mentor, Mr. Oliver T. Murdock. Mr. Murdock had been a Baltimore City Police Officer for over 30 years. He foot-patrolled one of the worst neighborhoods in Baltimore: Cherry Hill.

Mr. Murdock earned the respect of every thug, wannabe thug, and family in Cherry Hill. He would come and talk to you and tell you not to be there when he walked back around. If you were there when he came back, he would have a few words with you and take you home. If you committed a crime and he saw you, first he would tell you not to run. If you ran, you suffered the consequences of being caught, then you were taken home, after being taught a lesson in respect and obedience.

Officer Murdock was a very athletic and caring man. He was a good boxer, good in judo and karate, and could outrun most. So when he caught you, it was in your best interest not to challenge him, just listen to him and let him take you home or to work. He would talk to your parents and then give them a job. He would have them deliver newspapers, handing out leaflets, washing cars—anything to get them off the street. This he would do before he went to work in the morning and/or after he got off work in the evening.

I met him while working for the Federal Protective Service and then we were classmates in the Plumbing Apprenticeship Program. He was 60 years old then and we all wondered why he was there. After talking to him and being around him at work, you discovered why he was there. He loved working, he loved teaching, but he especially loved people. Because he loved people, he would do anything in his power for you. He would give you the shirt off his back and give you his last penny if it would help you, especially young black men.

Chicken is one of the things I like to cook. I always knew that there was a lot to learn about cooking: seasonings, combinations of herbs and spices, cooking techniques, cuts of meat, what compliments what, etc. So I researched and visited culinary schools in Bangkok, Thailand, Bali, Indonesia, Saigon, Vietnam, Kuala Lumpur I, Malaysia, and Angeles City, Philippines.

I finally decided to enroll in a level two cooking class at the Emelita Wong Galang Culinary Arts Studio in Angeles City. The school was close to where I was staying and offered the basics that I was looking for. Some of the others only offered four-to six-year training programs and apprenticeships, far beyond what I wanted.

The only thing that I did not like was that the class only met once a week. However, I was still able to learn and practice the basic techniques of cutting and using knives along with other kitchen utensils, methods of cooking, herbs and spices, fragrances and aromas, temperature control, plating, etc. It was a fun and very interesting course. But it was also a tough 20 weeks.

There were only two men in a class of 11. I was the only foreigner and I didn't speak Tagalog. The instructors, as well as the other students, were good about speaking English most of the time. Even though I did not speak the native language, I pretty much held my own, especially when it came down to cooking, recipe creation, and baking were not my strong points. I had no imagination so I still have a great deal more to learn. I think the reason I made it through was that I learned that I had a desire to learn, building on things I learned from my momma while growing up, accompanied by life experiences.

Cooking, I think, is not completely about what you prepare to eat, but also the thought and love you put into preparing the meal. If you have a strong base and love what you are doing, you can get the rest to work for you. I learned in Masonry, you have to "learn to listen, so you listen to learn." Another instructor said, "Think it through before you begin."

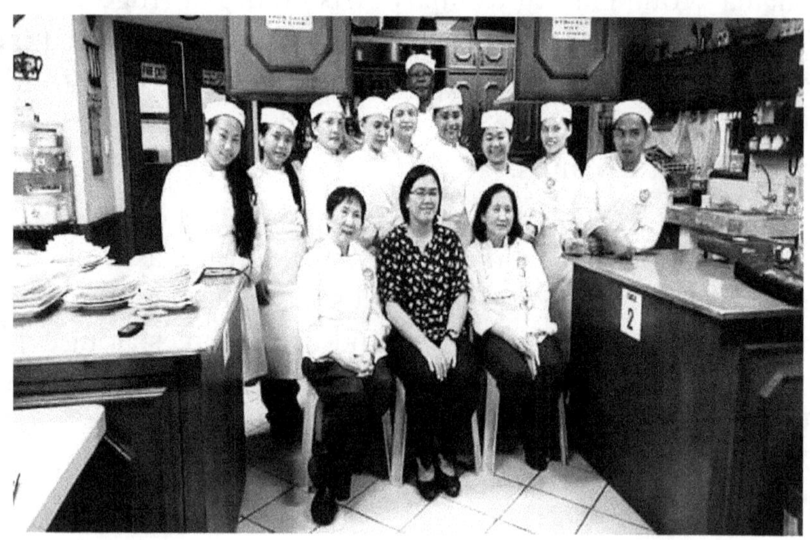

Graduation Day 2017

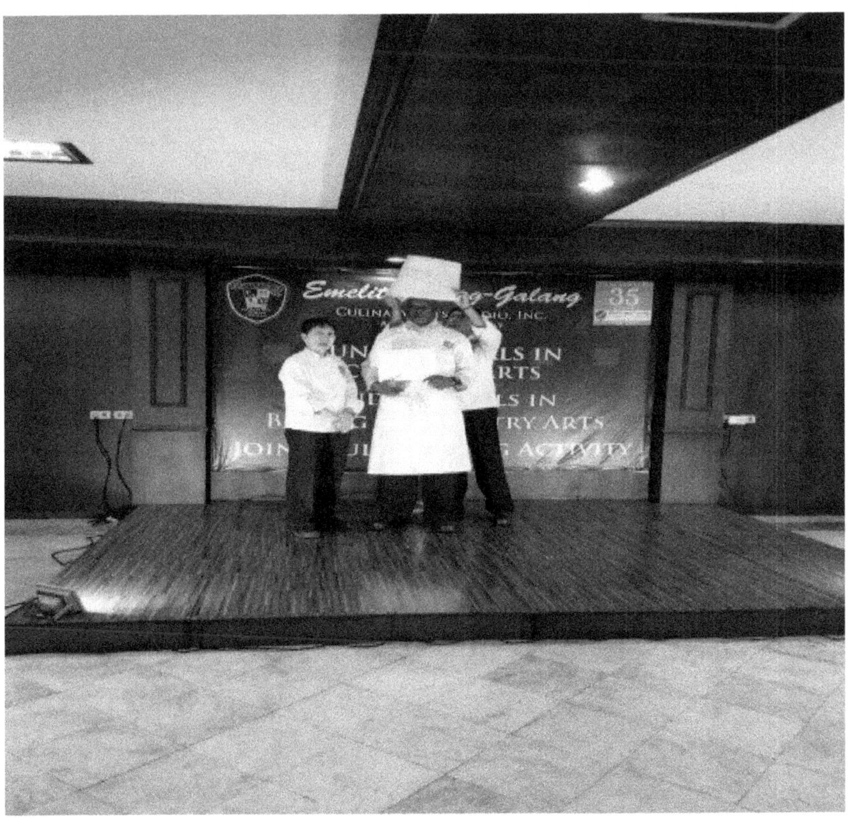

Being in the basic cooking class and being over 60, I now understood how Mr. Murdock felt being with all of us youngsters in the Plumbing Apprenticeship Program. When I had only about six months of experience, he'd had four years. Although they started to call me "Daddy," I developed a sense of responsibility to mentor those that sought my advice. I never avoided an opportunity to offer advice to those that did not take what they were doing seriously and were wasting their time and somebody else's money.

My classmates overall were raw and most of them had no kitchen experience. Their parents and significant others were investing in their futures and also trying to save their own stomachs. In the beginning, it was frightening, but in the end, we pulled through during our evaluation day.

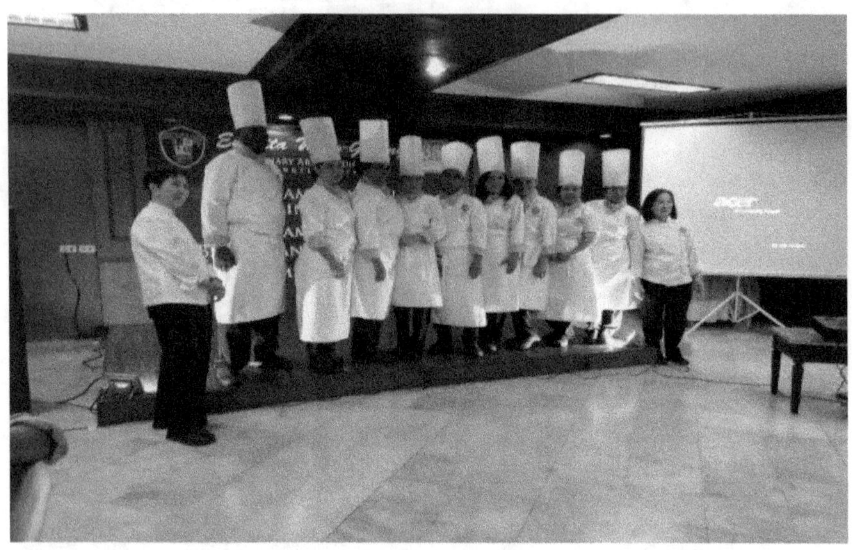

Our evaluation entailed preparing a seven-course meal to include appetizers and hors d'oeuvres with different ingredients; hot and cold sandwiches; soups, a salad, and whatever entrée they assigned you to cook and complete it with hot and cold desserts. It was just like the cooking shows on television where they give you a time limit to select your ingredients, prep them, cook, and serve everything.

I did not plan to take the evaluation. I was not there for any certifications, I just wanted to learn a little bit more about cooking. I always remained a gentleman in class. I would give the young ladies first choice on everything to work with and I would make do with whatever was left. They gave a one-day practice three days before the actual evaluation and I learned my lesson about those young ladies. I found out that they were all for themselves and, everybody else (especially this old foreign guy) did not matter. They took all the ingredients they could carry, even if their recipe did not call for it. They would not offer you anything to help you with your meal. I came up short on ingredients for my meal.

At the end of that day, I was exhausted and confused. I wanted to end it all right then. Talking to the instructor, she broke it all down to me and convinced me I was being too critical about it.

For the next three days, I studied and prayed. I put together four menus: beef, chicken, seafood, and pork to be ready for whatever the evaluator told me to prepare. I wrote everything out and left nothing to chance.

Once we got started on the day of the evaluation, I left the gentleman at the door and focused on my meal. There was no "Excuse me, may I get this? Can I use that?" Toward the end, they were coming to me to ask for things. I may sound cruel, but life is not always nice and polite.

The evaluator told me that I scored higher than most by understanding and doing the basic requirements where the other students concentrated on doing complicated and fancy meals. I was also able to explain my techniques and name my recipes. I achieved the Philippine National Culinary Level Two Certification. I Have **Almost Made It!**

Choices We Make in Life

The last thing I want to talk about deals with living a healthy life. All of my adult life I believed I was living a normal, healthy life and it probably was in some ways. I was active and fit. But I remember a friend of my family once told me that if I "did not smoke or drink and saved that money, I could become a millionaire." Well, I grew up around smoking and drinking; it was the norm. I looked up to my uncles and most of them either smoked or drank and some did both. My momma smoked for over 20 years. I don't remember when she stopped.

I got smart a lot faster when it came to cigarettes. When I was in high school, I started to smoke a little bit more to impress my friends and cigarettes were plentiful. Then I saw some of the stars and really fast athletes smoking so that just put the icing on the cake for me. I thought smoking would help make me faster!

My momma was working at the airport and would bring home small boxes of cigarettes and other goodies, so I always had a good supply of "smokes." At some point, we moved from Bryant Avenue to a house on Ocala Avenue only a couple of blocks away. Yes, I said a HOUSE with one family and a backyard! We never had a house to ourselves before.

One day during the Christmas holidays, my momma pulled me to the side and said, "I know you are out there smoking and drinking." I was shocked because I was always chewing gum to hide the odor. Then she said, "I would rather you do it here than out there in the street." I was happy and heartbroken at the same time because I could tell that I had broken her heart. I am so, so SORRY, momma!

My smoking only lasted for a short period of my young life. I continued to smoke while in the Corps. I trained hard almost every day with my new found friend, Michael Pope. One day Mike approached me about my smoking. He said, "We train hard and run all these miles and you come back and light up a cigarette. What's up with that?" I had no answer for him.

One day I decided that I would try to quit smoking by smoking a pipe. I went to the post exchange/PX and brought some fancy non-expensive pipes and flavored tobacco. I went home that weekend and was talking to momma about it. She had stopped smoking a few years before. Then she told me: "Son if it is something that you don't want to do, you will not do it."

After that talk, I never smoked again. For years I had nightmares about smoking and then it finally went away. This is another one of my smarter decisions I finally realized had to be made and it may have saved my life.

In high school, I started drinking. I remember during the riots after Dr. Martin Luther King had been killed, people had broken in and looted the neighborhood stores and bars owned by Whites. After they had been boarded up, my friends and I would go into one of the larger stores that sold alcohol and help ourselves to all the liquor and beer we could carry. We would sell what we could sell to the guys in other neighborhoods and have parties. It was during that time that I started drinking. From there, I started smoking. One of the main reasons was because I did not like the taste of Gordon's Gin.

When I first got into high school, I was very, very strong and athletic. My friend nicknamed me "Superman." That led me to my next great excuse to start smoking. I kept straining muscles so I came up with, "The Doctor told me I was over shaped so I needed to get out of shape to stop pulling muscles." I don't know how many of them believed it, but that was my story and I was sticking to it!

We had so much liquor stored in my basement that we could have opened our own store. We stored it in my basement because my momma would never come down there. We lived on the second and third floors on Bryant Avenue and the basement belonged to whoever lived on the first floor. That apartment was usually unrented.

One day I decided to play a big shot and impress my classmates by bringing a pint of Gordon's Gin to school. The plan was that we would all drink a little bit during lunchtime, just to get a little buzz going. I started pouring it into the bottle of orange soda we had, but I knew nothing about the ratio of alcohol to soda. I was thinking that it was about six of us, so one pint should not do that much to us. I also thought that one soda should have been enough.

I started rationing it out and the guys took one sip and started giving it back to me. I did not want to look like a chump so I drank all of their drinks and mine. That came up to be the whole pint of gin.

Lunch break was over and we had to go back to class. I went to my next class and then just sat in that hot room. The gin began to do its thing. The room started spinning, I started getting sleepy, and my stomach started feeling bad because I had not had anything to eat. Finally, I passed out. To this day I still don't remember how I got to the other classes or home that day. After that day, it was years before I ever drank any more Gordon's Gin. I also never took any liquor to school again.

That was just the start for me. Throughout my teenage years, we always found a way to get high—whether drinking alcohol, cough syrup, or drugs. I tried almost everything but my first choice was alcohol.

Drugs like acid and marijuana had also found their way into my neighborhood and were almost given away to us beginners. Guys coming back from Vietnam brought the most potent marijuana back and were treating everyone. This was their way of trying to get new clients and pushers.

One of my cousins gave me some acid. He also educated me on taking it and selling it. His first lesson for me was to never take it by myself. I took it a couple of times and it made me feel good. I started liking it.

One night I broke his first rule and one night took some by myself. That night was not good. I found myself about to jump from my 3rd-floor window. Once I realized that I was hallucinating, I caught myself and tied myself to my bed. That was my last time for acid.

My cousin had real nice clothes and he would let me wear them. I started feeling like I needed to earn some quick money to buy some "fine vines." He explained to me the business end of selling drugs. His last words to me were, "If you are not willing to accept the consequences, don't get in the game. It could cost you your life." I listened to what he said and never wanted to get into the business of selling drugs. I had friends who did and were found dead or ended up in jail. My cousin had to leave Baltimore to save his own life. I stuck to drinking.

 I continued to drink for the next 50 plus years of my life. I enjoyed drinking, especially gin. I was an occasional and social drinker for many years. During those years I raised my children, helped others, went to work every day, and completed college. I was able to party with the best of them and still tend to my affairs.

I taught and participated in football, karate, kickboxing, boxing, as well as other sports and physical activities. There were times when I went over the line and jeopardized my life by drinking and driving. That was not a good or smart thing to do. I never was arrested for drinking under the influence, but I did have some close calls, nearly wrecking my car. Luckily, I had sense enough to pull the car over and go to sleep.

I would party with my friends after all sporting events, sometimes the entire weekend. We drank in the middle of the week; we celebrated personal achievements, birthdays, holidays, or any other reason we could come up with to drink. We drank after my bouts, games, competitions, exams, a major training, or any other thing I thought significant enough to warrant a celebration drink. When I entertained the ladies, alcohol was the main course and really would flow.

All those years started catching up with me, affecting my internal organs. The doctors kept telling me mildly that my enzymes were at high levels, but I just associated it with drinking the night before. They never told me that I needed to stop drinking, so it was drinking as usual.

Finally, one doctor told me that I was in stage-four liver cirrhosis and I was having kidney dysfunctions. He flat out told me that I should stop drinking. I did not know what all those medical terms meant, but what came to my mind was my uncle had just died the month before from cirrhosis of the liver. This got my attention and I decided that even though I enjoyed drinking, it was not as important to me as living. This was a no-brainer!

I stopped drinking that day, May 2, 2019. Alcohol works on each of us differently, but the results can end up the same. I began eating more vegetables, drinking more water, exercising more, and taking the prescribed medication. After not drinking for three months and doing these things, my counts were returning to normal. I had the best check-up I had received in seven years.

The human body is complicated but is simply the machine that our Creator put together from the dust of the earth. Our lives are his gift to us to enjoy, if only for a short time. He gave it to us so we should enjoy it!

These were just a couple of the decisions that I think helped me to attain the station in life I am in now. There were many more and I am sure more to come as long as I keep living. **We Almost Made It!** does not mean it is over yet. I am sure God is not finished with me yet.

I MADE IT

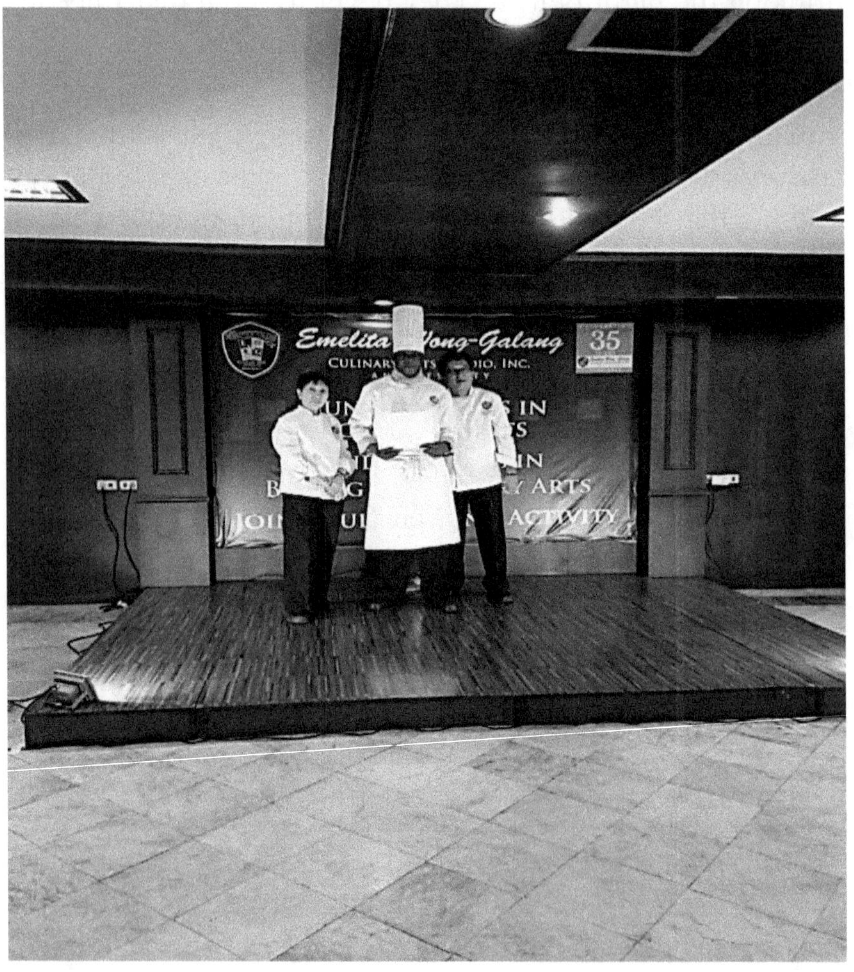

1977-White Belts

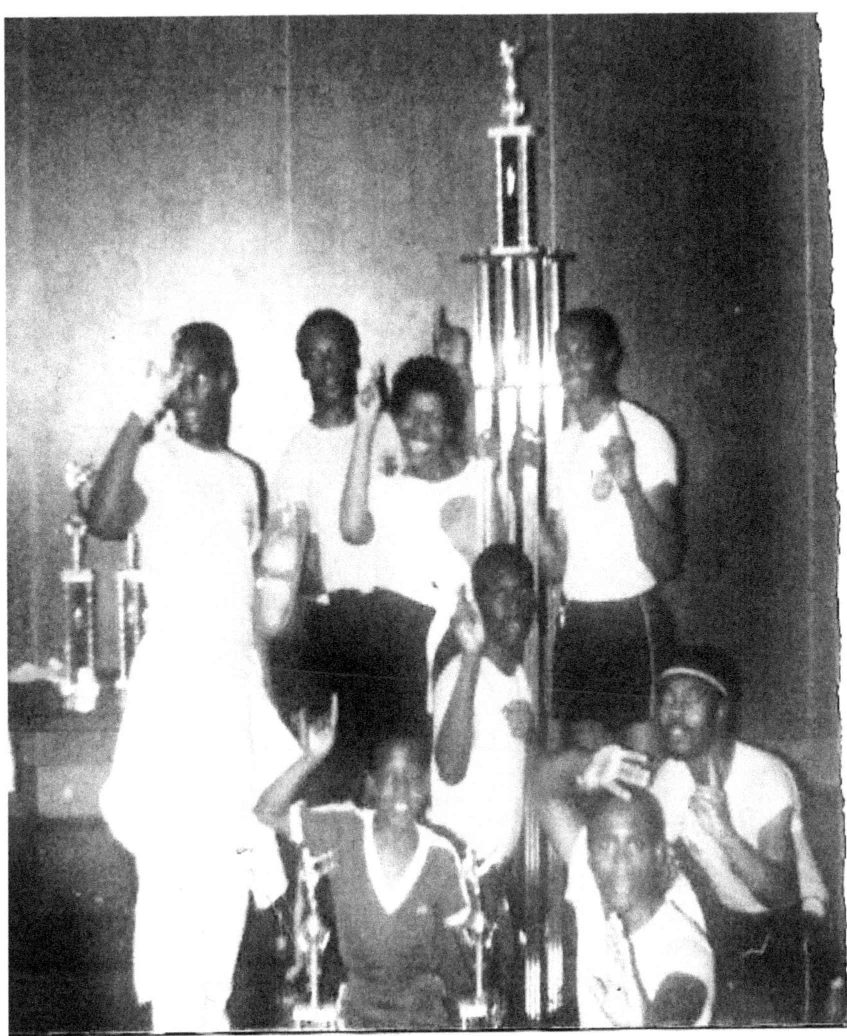

40 years Reunion- 1977-2017

Front Row: Jayden Marks, Pete Spencer, Warren "Wonder Boy" Watkins, Brenda "Ms. Gail" Fernandez, Yvette Muhammad, Sarah Taylor, Ms. Thelma, Minister Elizabeth Stemley, Mike "Grump" Arter

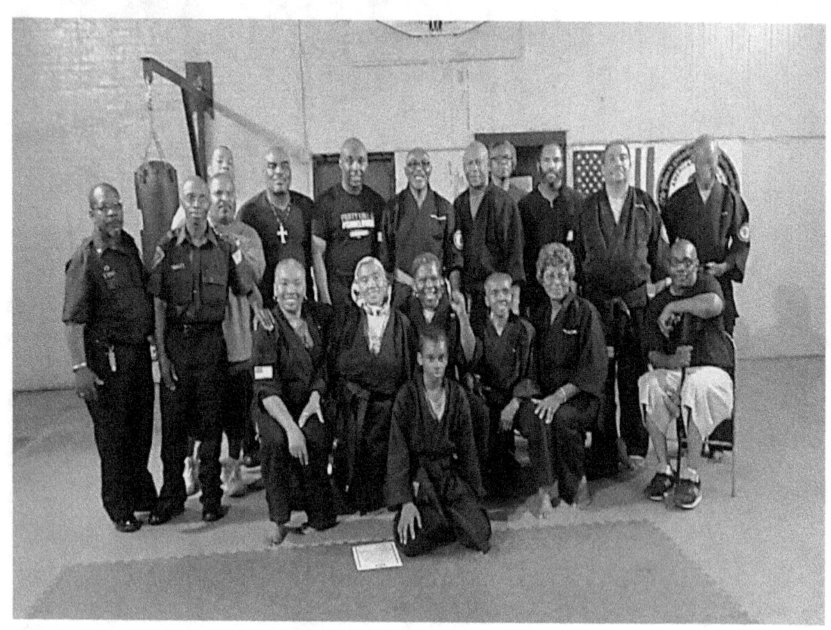

Back Row: Wytashe Miller, Wayne "Smokey" Carter, Steave "Awesome" Williams, Sensei Leroy "Superfeet" Taylor, Sylvester "Ironman" Cash, Arthur "Chippy" Cage, Gary Ball, Jose Fernandez, Atlas Washington

L-R: Wytashe, Boy Wonder, Smokey, Sensei, Cash, Steave "Awesome"

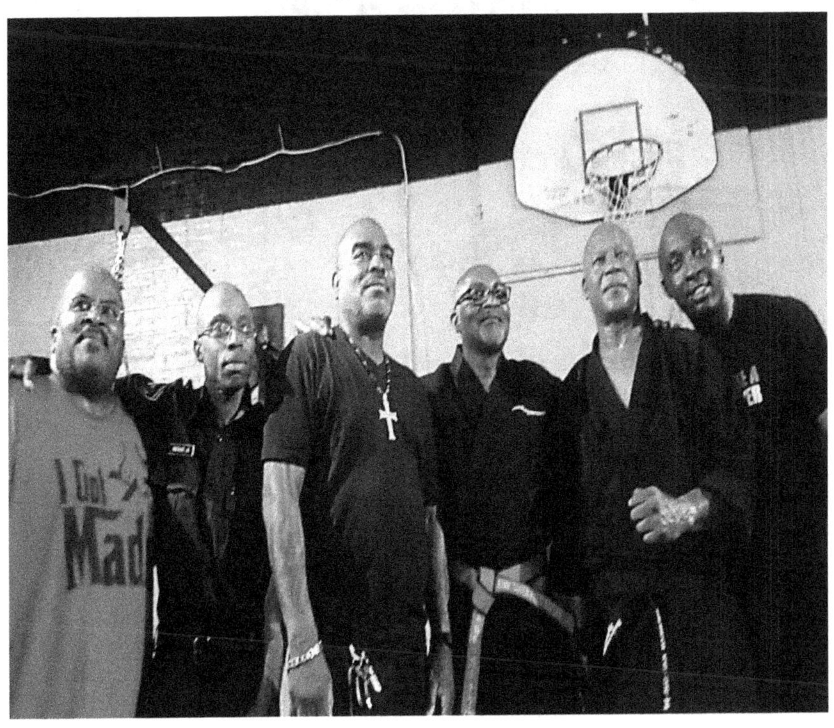

Aikido Shodan Exam 2016

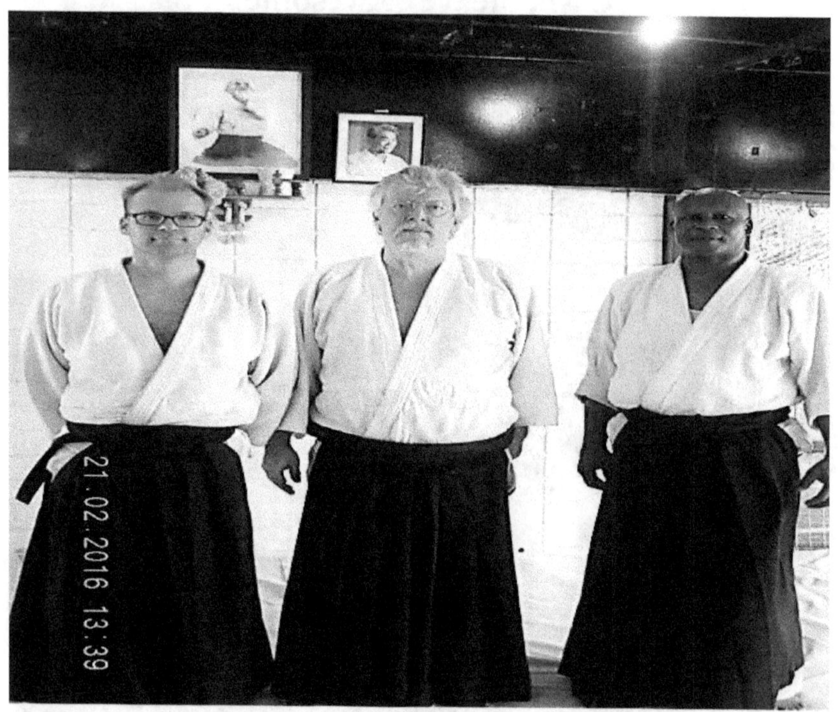

Aikido and Iaido Class 2017

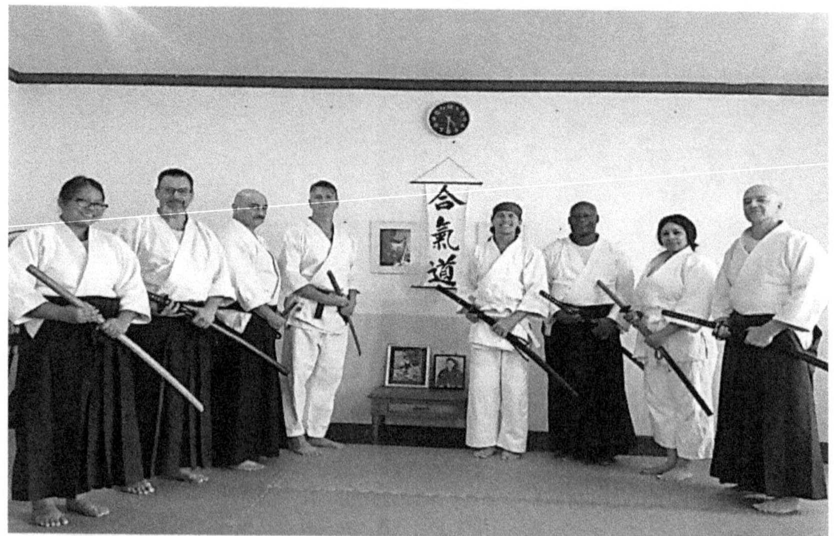

Isshinryu Karate 2015 Class

Tom, Erik, Dave Sensei, Cash, Pat

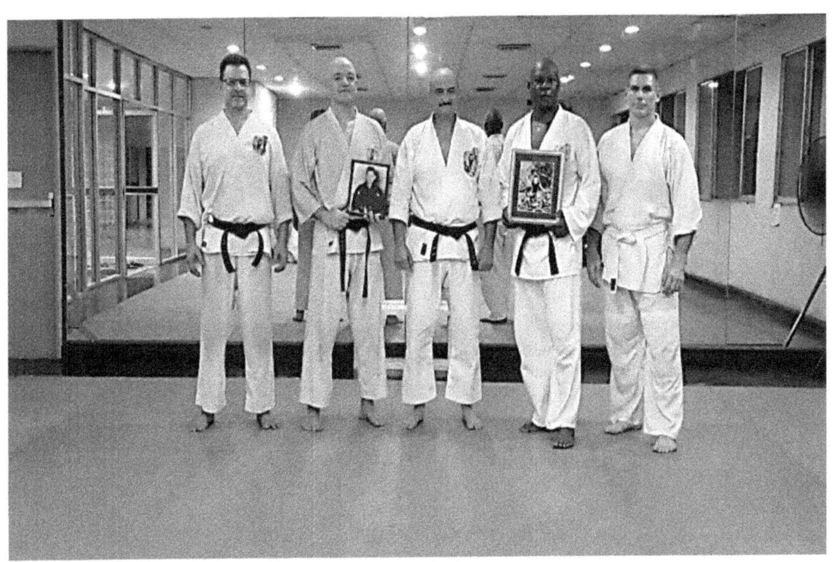

We Almost Made It

We Almost Made It does not mean that the journey is over. This phrase is meant to show the reader that there is always a chance in life to execute your ambitions and dreams. This is in no way intended to make any grand claims about how I ended up the way I am, but hopefully, it will inspire those that read it and let them know that the road to success in life is not easy, but you can make it!

When I look back over my life, I feel that it was only by the grace of God and my mother, family, friends, and others that I met during my journey that I made it this far. I would like others to know that you also have to leave your mark on the world. I hope by me sharing our experiences, you may be able to realize that you can make it too!

You may not get where you want to go in the long run, but you will get a lot further than where you were at the time when you started your journey! I only pray that this story will still end up the way I planned it and help someone else in their life. I would like to help them see that there is always hope. Even when you feel that there is no hope, keep the FAITH!

I was always told, "Faith is the substance of things not seen but hoped for." So when things seem lost and times seem bad; when things are not going the way you planned or thought it would be, keep the faith and get back up. Try a little harder and seek guidance from your God! "Go to the Upper Room" or your "prayer closet." Look up to the heavens and seek guidance from your God. Do this before seeking guidance from man.

I have now retired from Federal Service and have confirmation of the value in the things I have seen and experienced along the journey of life. This is the hardest retirement of all. Retirement from Federal Service after 41+ years of getting up and having somewhere to be. Retirement from 41+ years of having to answer to a job, to the "man". 41+ years of not being in control of your time. Always having to be here at this time, be there at that time, and don't be late!

I thought that retiring from competition was hard, but at least I could still coach and train guys. I was still competing, not only against those that came up with me (mostly the other trainers and coaches) but with the world and its hardships and unfairness. I could still go to the office/gym each week and work out, encouraging, training, motivating and mentoring young fighters and karate practitioners, hopefully giving them the knowledge to be successful in the outside world.

What we do and teach becomes a part of their lives, not just a fad. Each student that we teach, train, and coach remains our responsibility for the rest of our lives (and I hope their lives). You are probably wondering why I say this?

Well, I explain this to every one of my students before accepting them as students. I explained to all of them, that I am responsible for them for the rest of their lives and their actions from this point on. I am not only responsible for them when they come to the Dojo, but also when they are at home, in school, at work, and in play.

I hope that they will always be able to confide in me and I will always try to be available to them. When they first sign up they do not understand that we as instructors are giving them a very special weapon. That weapon is the knowledge of life and death. This is not just martial arts knowledge for competitive karate, boxing, and kickboxing for use only in the ring, but knowledge to take with you into the world, to grow and live by.

This being understood, we as Sensei, Coach, or Trainer, hold a great responsibility to the world. It is our responsibility to teach our students the right way. Teaching them the proper way of using what we have taught them in the dojos, in the gyms, and in the world, we share with others that do not have our knowledge.

This concern and responsibility were manifested one day when I asked one of my 6-year-old students what he would do if someone grabbed him in his collar. The answer I got from him was astounding. I had to go back and re-evaluate my program and change the wording I was using to explain techniques. I also started thinking more about why I was teaching karate. From that time on, I broke it down into these four areas, which we have our students learn and repeat after each class in the hope that it will carry over into their lives.

1.   **One purpose of karate is to instill self-discipline.**

2.   **One purpose of karate is to instill self-confidence.**

3.   **One purpose of karate is to strengthen the mind and the body.**

4.   One purpose of karate is to be a means of protection, knowledge that is never to be misused.

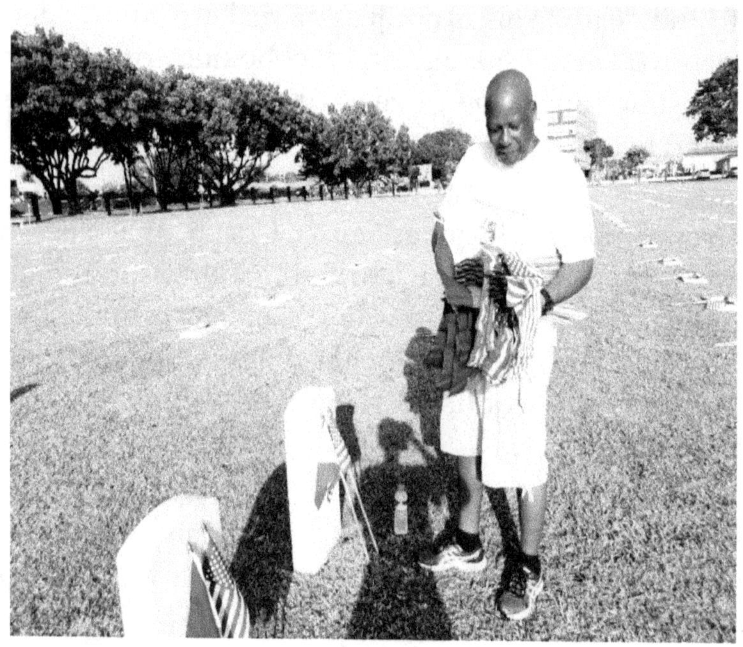

Today, I also go to the Veteran's Cemetery in the Philippines each year and place flags over the graves of our Heroes and Brothers!

Thank You, Lord, for all these opportunities to serve you and my fellow man!